Dalí

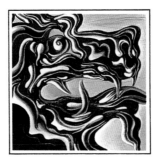

THE LIFE AND WORKS OF

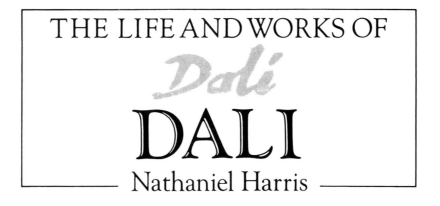

DALI

Nathaniel Harris

A Compilation of Works from the
BRIDGEMAN ART LIBRARY

This is a Parragon Book
This edition published in 2003

Parragon, Queen Street House, 4 Queen Street, Bath BA1 1HE, UK

ISBN 1-85813-656-3

Printed in China

Editor: Alexa Stace
Designer: Robert Mathias

The publishers would like to thank Joanna Hartley
at the Bridgeman Art Library for her invaluable help.

DALI 1904-1989

Dalí

SALVADOR DALI WAS A GREAT ARTIST who was also a great self-publicist and showman. The combination was an irresistible formula for success. Dalí the showman, his moustaches arrogantly upturned, became a familiar figure to millions who had never been near an art gallery. In this guise he seemed always at the ready with a paean of slightly absurd self-praise or a string of wittily inconsequential remarks which might or might not be profundities. But those who scorned Dalí as a charlatan had to come to terms with the fact that he created a host of dazzling images, some of which, like the soft watches in *The Persistence of Memory* (pages 20-21), have entered the general consciousness of our culture.

Dalí was a Spaniard, born on 11 May 1904 in the little Catalan town of Figueras. In a sense, Dalí's entire world consisted of Figueras, the Ampurdán plain in which it stands, the little fishing village of Cadaqués just beyond the mountains, and nearby Port Lligat where he built his home. These are the settings for the great majority of his works, even when their foreground is occupied with a crucifixion or a civil war.

Though he acquired more than his share of childhood neuroses and sexual fixations, Dalí came from a solidly middle-class family. They had wealthy and cultivated friends who encouraged the young Dalí and kept him unusually well informed about the dramatic developments taking place in the world of art. He was already artistically well-equipped when he went to study painting in Madrid (1921-6), and the period was more important for the close friendships he formed with the poet Lorca and the director Luis Buñuel, with whom Dalí made the celebrated film *Un Chien Andalou* (1929).

From about 1927 Dalí was increasingly drawn to Surrealism. This Paris-based movement, influenced by the relatively new psychoanalytical theories of Sigmund Freud, created works dictated by the unconscious mind through dreams, automatic writing and other procedures aimed at freeing the artist from the tyranny of rationality.

In 1929 Dalí established himself as a member of the group with the help of Gala Eluard, the woman who became not only his lover and wife but his 'minder' and muse. Initially, Gala seems to have saved Dalí from a serious mental crisis, and without her support and belief in his genius he might never have achieved so much; on the other hand it was Gala, growing increasingly greedy and extravagant, who later encouraged him to commercialize and often trivialize his art. Dalí himself promoted an ever more extravagant cult of Gala, whose many appearances in his work culminated in almost goddess-like images.

Dalí painted his most famous, and probably his best, works in the decade 1929-39, using a 'paranoiac-critical method' of his own devising. It involved various forms of irrational association, notably using images which changed according to the viewer's perception of them, so that a group of fighting soldiers could suddenly be seen as a woman's face. A distinctive feature of Dalí's art was that, however bizarre the imagery, it was always painted in an impeccable 'academic' technique, with 'photographic' accuracy of a kind that most of his avant-garde artist contemporaries regarded as outmoded.

Towards the end of the 1930s Dalí was becoming known in the United States, where attitudes towards artistic innovation were less conservative than in the Old World. The outbreak of World War II and the German victory over France in 1940 prompted Dalí to flee to the United States, where he stayed for eight years. America provided abundant opportunities for Dalí to use his talents, and also brought out his exhibitionist side. He became a super-celebrity, staging 'happenings' long before the term was invented, and eventually even starring in TV commercials.

However, Dalí also continued to work hard and seriously, remaining prolific as an artist, designer and writer. He lived to become an icon of the hippie generation and to create a fantastic personal monument in the form of the Dalí Museum at Figueras, a total environment filled with bizarrely inventive objects and murals.

Dalí's later years were overshadowed by a degree of estrangement from Gala, although he was shattered by her death in 1982. Subsequently there was mounting concern about the number of fake works in circulation that were attributed to Dalí. He himself was partly to blame, since it was clear that he had been induced to sign hundreds, perhaps thousands, of sheets of blank paper which could obviously be put to illicit uses. Virtually a living ghost, he lingered on until his death on 29 January 1989. He is buried in the Dalí Museum in his native town.

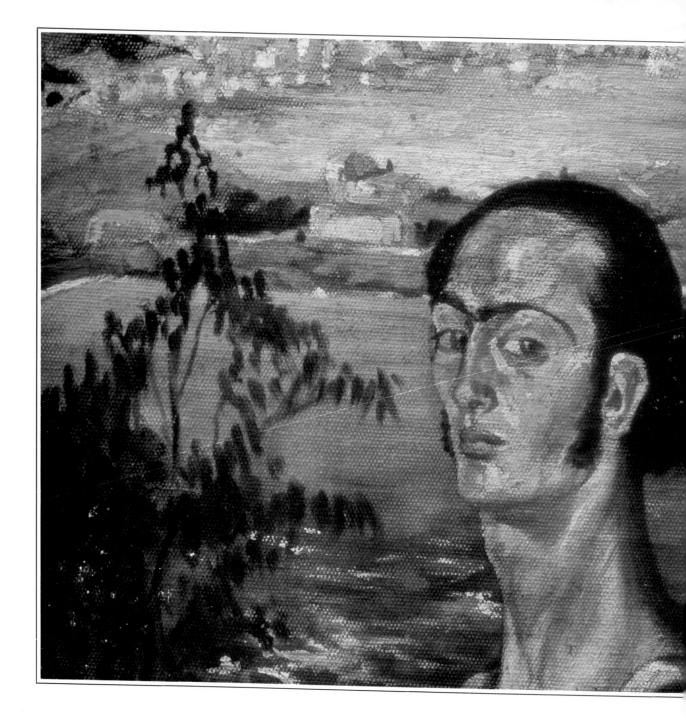

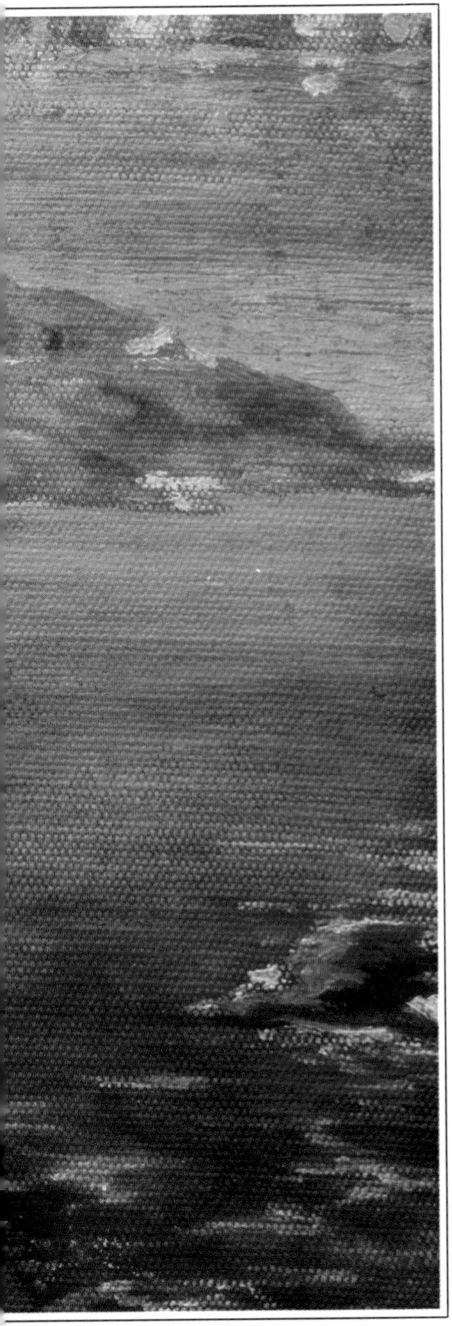

◁ **Self-portrait with Raphaelesque Neck** 1921

Oil on canvas

THIS WAS PAINTED when Dalí was only seventeen, although he makes himself look somewhat older and uncharacteristically rugged. 1921 was the year when his mother died (according to Dalí, one of his most traumatic experiences) and when he left home for the first time to enrol as as student at the San Fernando Academy in Madrid. The rather severe, challenging self-portrait has a misleading air of machismo, probably intended to conceal Dalí's extreme timidity, as did his later and better known self-image as a mustachioed dandy and prankster. The painting technique, although accomplished, is still derivative, the brushwork and colour scheme showing the influence of Impressionism, Pointillism and other 'modern' movements which Dalí would soon reject in favour of a meticulously accurate 'academic' style. The background of the picture shows the sea, the Costa Brava coastline and the little fishing village of Cadaqués which were to figure so largely in Dalí's life and work.

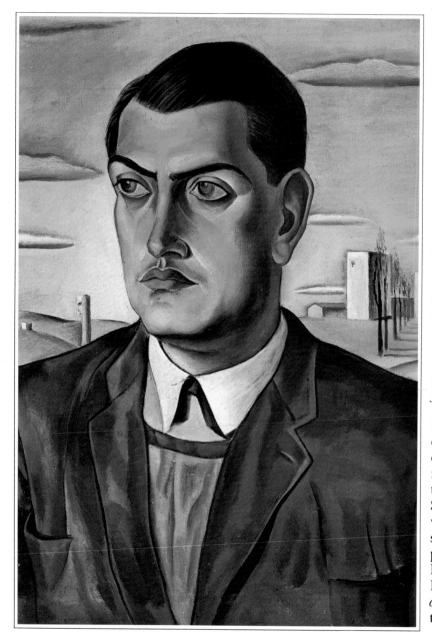

◁ **Portrait of
Luis Buñuel** 1924

Oil on canvas

DURING HIS YEARS AS a student
(1921-6), Dalí lodged in a large
hostel in Madrid, the
University Residence, where
he formed close friendships
with two fellow-students who
would also become famous:
Federico García Lorca, Spain's
greatest 20th-century poet,
and the distinguished film-
maker Luis Buñuel. The
rituals and eccentricities
cultivated by the threesome
had a permanent influence on
Dalí's private mythology and
public self-image. In the later
1920s, student cameraderie
gave way to rivalries and
jealousies, especially between
Lorca and Buñuel. In 1929
Buñuel helped Dalí to
establish himself in Paris and
collaborated with him in
making *Un Chien Andalou,* now
the most celebrated of
Surrealist films; the scene in
which a girl's eye is abruptly
sliced with a razor still has the
power to make audiences gasp.
Dalí's collaboration with
Buñuel on a second film, *L'Age
d'Or,* was less harmonious, and
the friendship faded away.

▷ **Portrait of the Artist's Father** 1925

Oil on canvas

DON SALVADOR DALI, the notary of Figueras, was a man of strong personality who deeply influenced his painter son, mainly by evoking in the younger Dalí an intense and virtually lifelong reaction against everything he stood for. Don Salvador's commanding presence, and Dalí's helpless resentment, can be sensed in this and other portrait studies. In childhood Dalí rebelled through bedwetting, tantrums and bad performance at school; later, he deliberately failed to pass the final examination at his art college and gain the qualifications that would have assured him a 'respectable' future. After a complete estrangement between 1929 and 1934, Dalí and his father were reconciled, but the relationship remained an uneasy one.

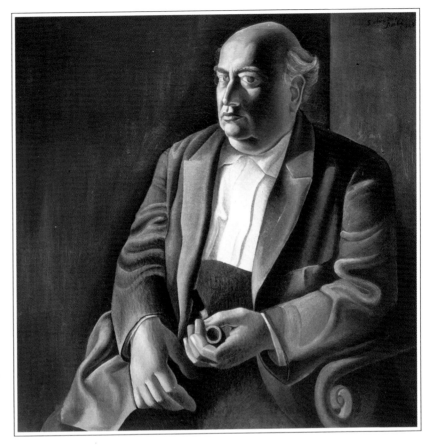

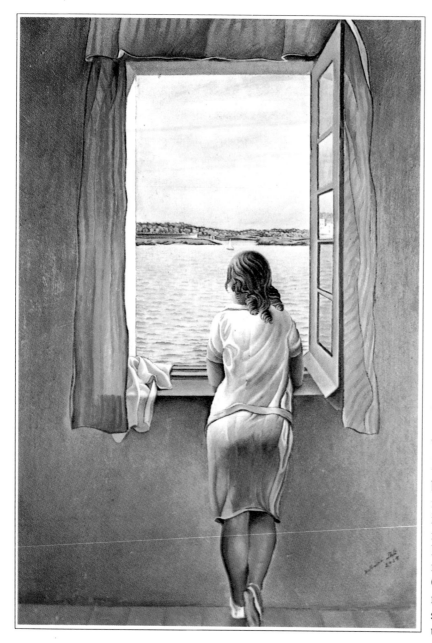

◁ **Girl Standing at a Window** 1925

Oil on canvas

THE GIRL IN THIS PAINTING is Dalí's sister Ana Maria, who posed for several portraits in the summer of 1925. As in the equally well-known *Girl Seated* and *Woman at the Window in Figueras* (page 15), she is shown from behind so that her face is concealed; an oddity of Dalí's, particularly in evidence at this time, that has been given various psychological interpretations. The blanking out of the human element creates an effect curiously at variance with the holiday mood suggested by the glimpse of the river and the picture's notable lightness and clarity. The painting was shown as part of Dalí's first one-man exhibition at the Delmau Gallery in Barcelona, where it was seen and admired by Picasso. Ana Maria mothered the hopelessly impractical and sexually fearful Dalí, and was effectively his only female model until he met his wife-to-be Gala Eluard; Gala took over the role of model in an equally exclusive spirit, earning Ana Maria's undying enmity.

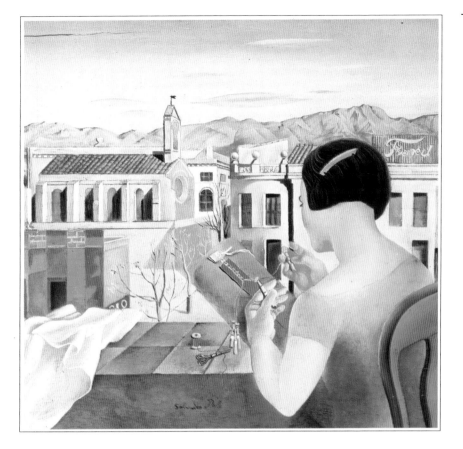

△ **Woman at the Window in Figueras** c 1926

Oil on canvas

IN THIS CHARMING PICTURE a woman sits making lace on a balcony overlooking the town square. Her equipment is shown in impeccable detail, and the scene can be interpreted as a Dalí counterpart to *The Lacemaker*, by the 17th-century Dutch artist Jan Vermeer. This painting became one of Dalí's obsessions, and visual references to it often crop up in his work. The treatment including the woman's modishly short, glossily highlighted hair is reminiscent of a magazine illustration in the reigning art deco style. In the background stand the buildings of Figueras, from first to last an important presence in Dalí's life: he was born and brought up there, his works were first exhibited at the town's municipal theatre, which he would later transform into a Dalí museum, and he was finally interred beneath its dome.

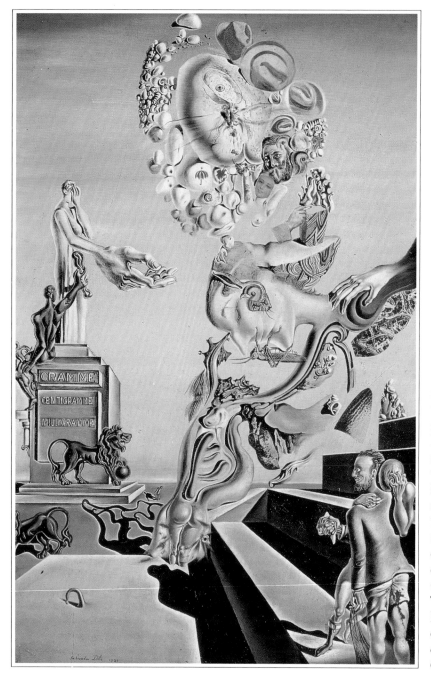

◁ **The Lugubrious Game** 1929

Oil and collage on canvas

BY THE LATE 1920s Dalí had embraced Surrealism and was developing the 'paranoiac-critical method' with which he plundered his psyche for images and associations. *The Lugubrious Game* (also known as *Dismal Sport*) was painted at Cadaqués in the summer of 1929, in preparation for Dalí's first one-man exhibition in Paris. Like several other works of the period, its subjects were masturbation, made overt by the statue's huge hand and Dalí's sexual fears and fixations. Among the objects in the spiralling column on the right is an image of Dalí himself, his mouth covered by a grasshopper, a creature of which he had an intense, irrational horror. Sexual and scatalogical images abound. *The Lugubrious Game* became the centrepiece of Dalí's extremely successful Parisian exhibition at the Goemans Gallery in November 1929. The painting was bought by his future patron, the Vicomte de Noailles, who hung it in his dining-room between works by Cranach and Watteau.

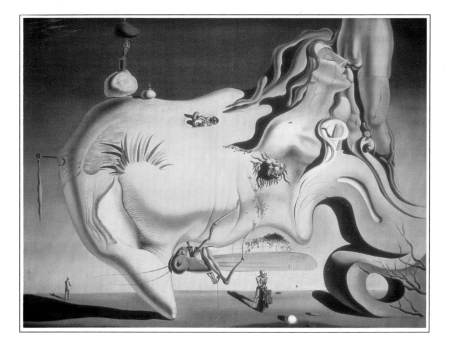

△ **The Great Masturbator** 1929

Oil on canvas

THE TITLE OF THIS PAINTING makes explicit the subject of *The Lugubrious Game* (page 14); Dalí himself described it as 'the expression of my heterosexual anxiety'. In 1929 he was still a virgin, inhibited by deep-seated fears of female sexuality and anal obsessions. Although these never left him, he seems for some time to have had a relatively normal sexual relationship with Gala Eluard, who left her husband, the poet Paul Eluard, for Dalí and eventually married him. *The Great Masturbator* was painted after their relationship had begun, but before they had unequivocally joined forces. According to Dalí, it was inspired by a 19th-century picture of a woman smelling an arum lily. Dalí moved the lily, replacing it with a well-endowed male figure. Woman, lily and male figure emerge from the strange 'Dalí' head which had already appeared in *The Lugubrious Game*. The small figure on his own, and the man making love to a rock shaped like a woman, point up the theme of solitary male fantasy.

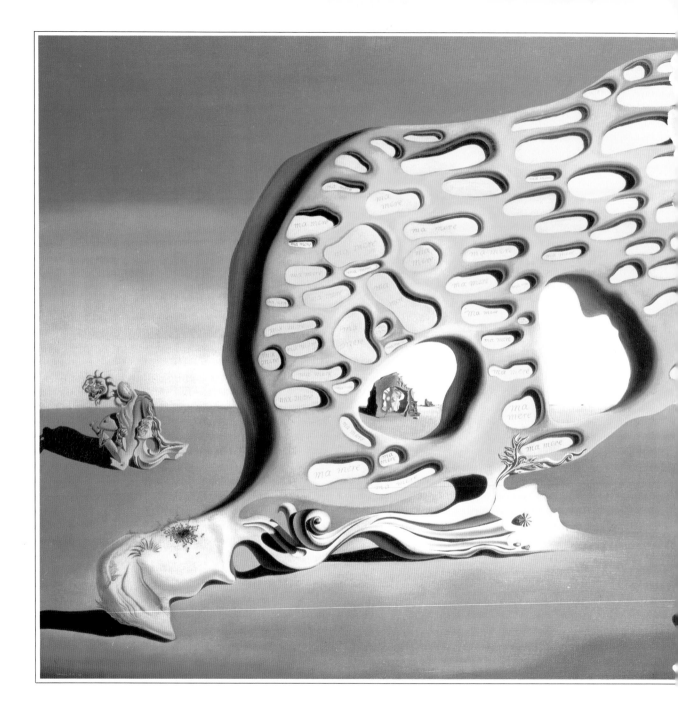

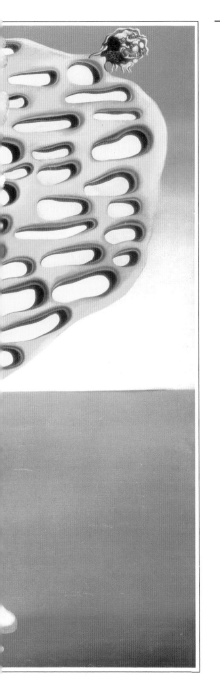

◁ **The Enigma of Desire:
My Mother, My Mother, My Mother** 1929

Oil on canvas

LIKE *The Lugubrious Game* and *The Great Masturbator* (pages 14 and 15), this painting features a pallid, apparently soft head of Dalí himself, evidently asleep and presumably dreaming. It has been plausibly suggested that the shape of the head derived from the extraordinary rock formations around Cadaqués, where Dalí made his home. Here, however, the head and its familiar attachment of curlicued furniture are quite small, while the canvas is dominated by a large compartmented and pierced object reminiscent of a brain; many, but not all, of the 'cells' are labelled *ma mère* (my mother), doubtless because room had to be left for other obsessions! Ants, lion heads, a grasshopper, a sea creature with a shell, and other objects from Dalí's private world are present, along with two more obviously Freudian images: a hand holding a (castrating?) knife and a wounded female torso.

Detail

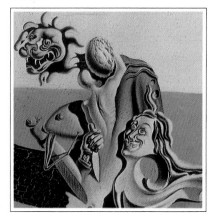

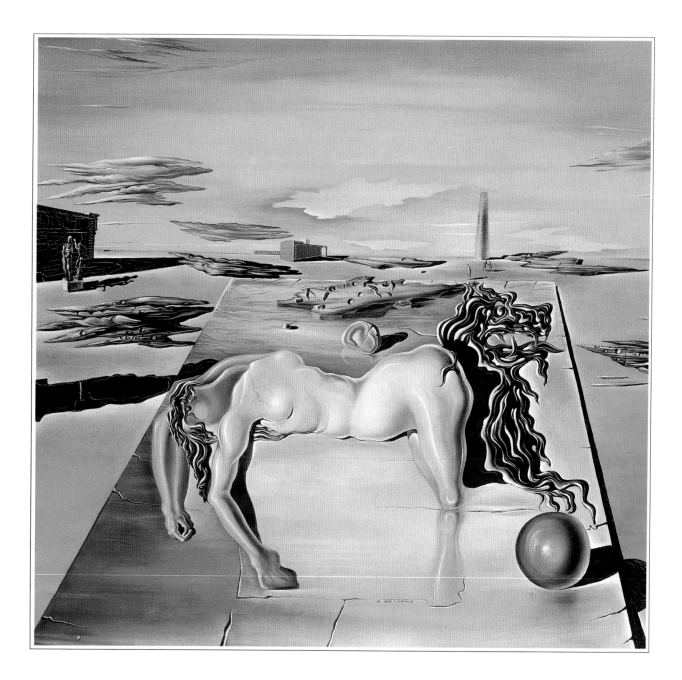

◁ Invisible Sleeping Woman, Horse, Lion 1930

Oil on canvas

DALÍ'S VERBAL DESCRIPTIONS of his 'paranoiac-critical method' leave most readers little wiser; but the personal effectiveness of the 'method' can hardly be questioned, since it enabled Dalí to tap his unconscious and produce chains of potent, startling images. By 1930 he was 'continuing the paranoiac advance' by devising a technique of registering multiple images which could be 'read' in different ways. This picture is an early example of a triple image: at its centre is a reclining female nude, but the maned head to her right transforms the image into that of a lion, while a shift of focus to the left brings out the image of a horse, its head formed by the woman's left hand and arm. This was a landmark in Dalí's development, signalled by the fact that he made no less than three versions of the picture: one was destroyed in a cinema foyer by right-wing demonstrators objecting to the Dalí-Buñuel film *L'Age d'Or.*

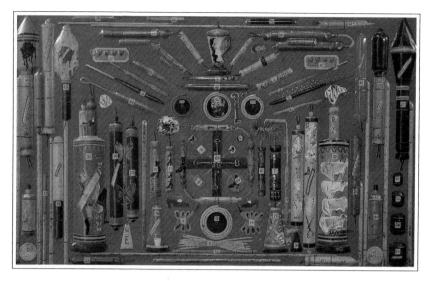

△ Fireworks 1930-1

Embossed and enamelled pewter

ALSO KNOWN AS *The Mad Associations Board, Fireworks* was originally a board advertizing the wares of a fireworks firm, amusingly transformed by the little paintings in oils which Dalí added to it. One of Surrealism's most audacious contributions to art was the 'found object' *(objet trouvé),* which might be a banal manufactured item (such as the bottle rack exhibited by Marcel Duchamp) or, more usually, a strikingly shaped natural object such as a rock. A further development was the 'assisted' found object, worked on by the artist; Dalí was characteristically inventive in creating Surrealist objects, which included not only *Fireworks* but a notorious *Lobster Telephone* and a sofa shaped like the red lips of the film star Mae West.

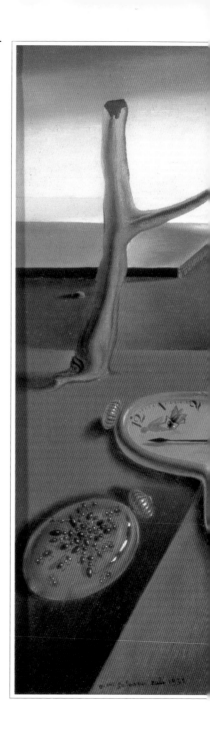

▷ **The Persistence of Memory** 1931

Oil on canvas

THIS QUITE SMALL PAINTING (24 x 33 cm/9^1/$_2$ x 13 in) is probably the most celebrated of all Dalí's works. The flaccidity of the hanging, slithering watches is a brilliant concept, more effective than many more sensational distortions in undermining our belief in a natural, rule-bound order of things. The imagery reaches into the unconscious, evoking the seemingly universal human preoccupation with time and memory. Dalí himself is present, in the form of the dormant head which had already appeared in *The Lugubrious Game* (page 14) and other paintings. Characteristically, he claimed that the idea for the painting came to him while he was meditating upon the nature of Camembert cheese; the Port Lligat background was already painted, so it took him only a couple of hours to finish the painting. When Gala, who had been out at the cinema, returned, she correctly predicted that no one who had seen *The Persistence of Memory* would ever forget it.

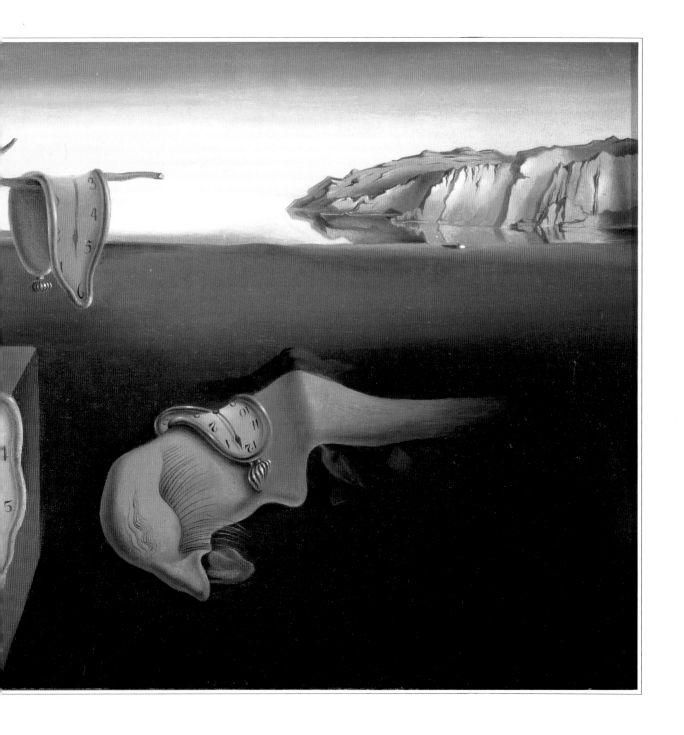

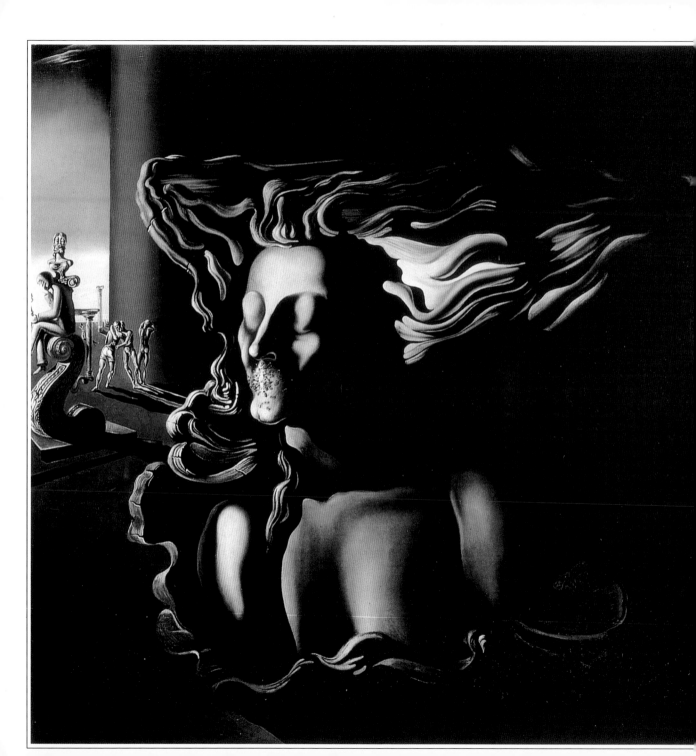

◁ **The Dream** 1931

Oil on canvas

THE DREAM WAS PAINTED at a time when Dalí and Gala were uncomfortably lodged in a fisherman's hut at Port Lligat which they were later to transform into a luxurious, labyrinthine home: not the least of the magical metamorphoses in which Dalí specialized. Paradoxically, in 1931 Dalí's pictures were having a considerable impact on the art world, while he was still finding it hard to make ends meet. At Port Lligat he worked untiringly, producing masterpieces such as this hauntingly atmospheric dreamscape. The image of a face without a mouth can be traced back to *Un Chien Andalou*, the classic Surrealist film made in 1929 by Dalí and Luis Buñuel; in it, the main male character literally wipes his lips away, in a gesture that was patently intended to be one of sexual menace. Dalí's eerie, claustrophobic dream world now looks familiar and 'natural' – perhaps because it belongs to the universal unconscious, or perhaps because images created by him have now been universally absorbed.

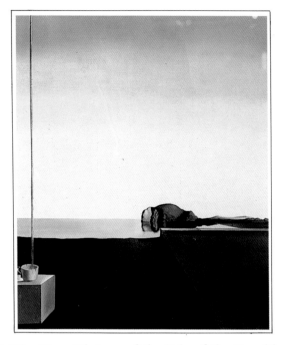

△ **The True Picture of the Isle of the Dead by Arnold Bocklin at the Hour of the Angelus** 1932

Oil on canvas

ARNOLD BOCKLIN (1827-1901) was a German Symbolist painter whose best known work, *The Isle of the Dead* (1880), was given its title by a dealer. Bocklin himself simply called it 'a picture to dream over', leaving the viewer to determine its meaning – an attitude close to the Surrealists' hearts. The relationship between the painting that inspired Dalí and his own 'Bocklin' canvas remains appropriately problematic. Something of Bocklin's romantic melancholy and taste for evening light lingers in Dalí's work, but he has replaced the lushness of the German artist's tree-crowded island with bare rocks, and the cup and the tall rod rising out of its bowl of course belong to the universe of Surrealism.

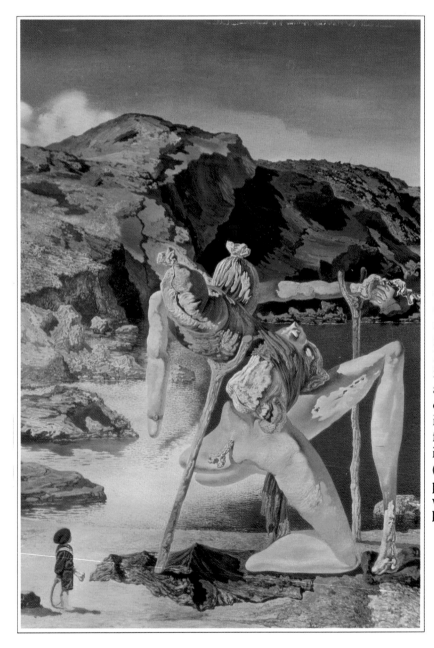

◁ **The Spectre of Sex Appeal** 1932

Oil on canvas

HUGE AND DECAYING on the beach, the rickety, propped-up figure of *Sex Appeal* is not a pretty sight; sex-appal might be a more appropriate term for this random collection of limbs, tenuously attached to a torso composed of sacks and ragged wrappings. The head merges into the rocks in a typical Dalí double image, and the amputated and ravaged extremities suggest the after-effects of cannibalism, an idea always closely linked with sex in Dalí's mind. According to his own account, the small boy in the sailor suit is Dalí at the age of six, holding a hoop in one hand and an ossified penis in the other. The identical figure reappears 35 years later in *The Hallucinogenic Toreador* (page 78). The cove is a real place, close to Cadaqués, which Dalí had probably known from his childhood.

▷ **Eggs on a Dish
without the Dish** 1932

Oil on canvas

THERE IS NO ENGLISH
equivalent to the punning
French title of this picture:
Oeufs sur le plat sans le plat.
Oeufs sur le plat, which literally
translates as 'eggs on the dish',
is actually the French term for
fried eggs; so 'eggs on the
dish' can in fact exist without a
dish, and even, as here,
improbably hang from a line
in mid-air, like bait on a
fisherman's hook. Dalí was
obviously pleased with the
joke, since he repeated it in an
identically titled canvas to
which he added a further
contradictory element by
actually putting in a dish! His
fondness for depicting two
near-identical fried eggs, set
close together and side by
side, suggests that he was also
aware of the slang use of *oeufs
sur le plat* to describe small
female breasts.

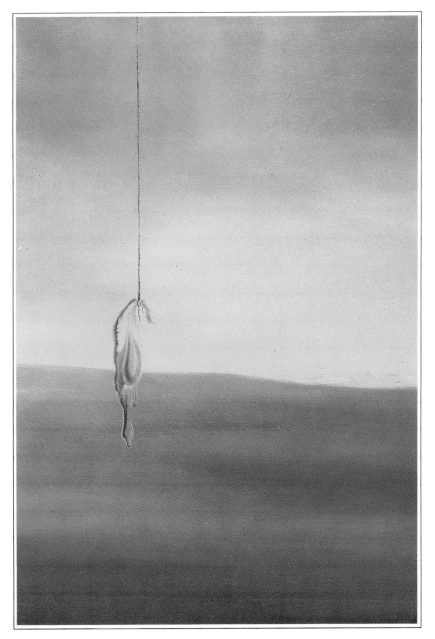

▷ **The Phantom Cart** 1933

Oils on panel

THIS IS A VERY SMALL PICTURE (19 x 24 cm/7¹/₂ x 9¹/₂ in), painted in oils on a panel. It is easy to overlook the fact that the central object is one of Dalí's multiple images, perhaps more successful than its equivalent in *Invisible Sleeping Woman, Horse, Lion* (page 18), since the illusion here requires no shift of focus to either side: the outlines of man and horse beneath the canopy of the cart can simply be reinterpreted as structures on the skyline of the town that the vehicle is approaching. So in *The Phantom Cart* the cart is actually less of a phantom than the creatures that draw and ride in it. The painting was based on Dalí's childhood memories of the day-long journeys between his home town in Figueras and the family house in the fishing village of Cadaqués, where he spent the summer holidays. For Dalí this was a period of freedom from constraint at home as well as at school, and this may help to account for the unusually serene atmosphere of the work.

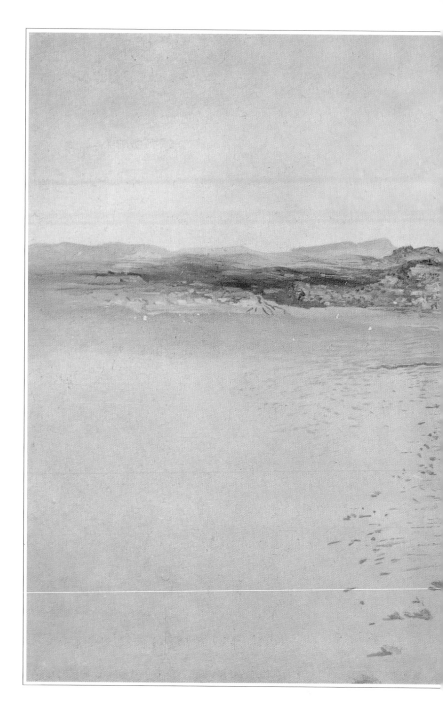

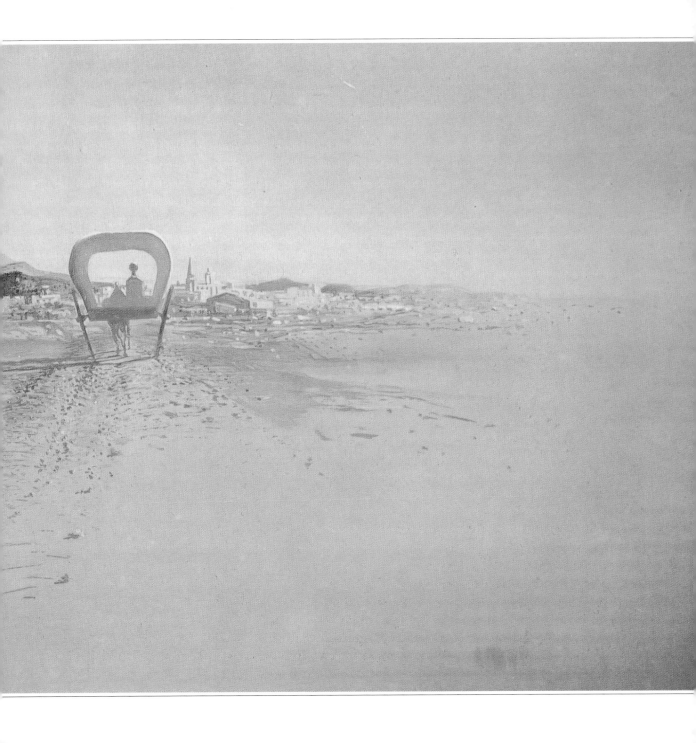

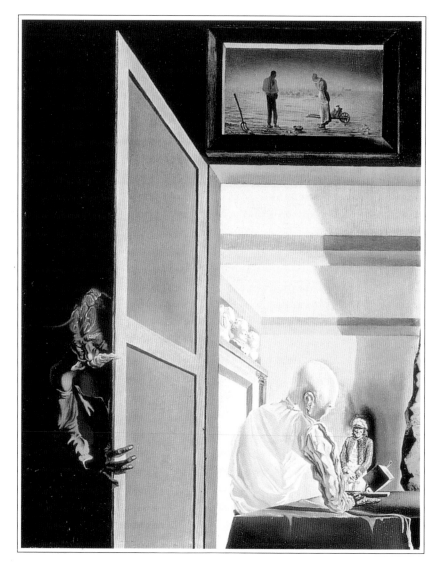

◁ **Gala and the Angelus of Millet Immediately Preceding the Arrival of the Conical Anamorphoses** 1933

Panel

IN THIS ENTERTAINING psychodrama, a grinning, trendily dressed Gala confronts a distorted figure of the Bolshevik leader of the Russian Revolution, Lenin. Maxim Gorki, the famous Russian writer associated with the Bolsheviks, eavesdrops, oblivious to the lobster on his head. Dalí seems to have viewed Lenin as a father-figure, and as such an enemy to be ridiculed. Gala, whose long partnership with Dalí was now firmly established, appears in the role of triumphant liberator. The picture over the doorway is Jean-François Millet's *The Angelus,* a popular 19th-century image of peasant goodness and piety. It became one of Dalí's prime obsessions, into which he read erotic meanings (for example, that the man's hat concealed a state of urgent sexual arousal). Here *The Angelus* is shown more or less as Millet painted it; later it would undergo various metamorphoses at Dalí's hands (pages 29, 30, 31).

▷ **The Architectonic Angelus of Millet** 1933

Oil on canvas

ONE OF A SERIES of remarkable paintings in which Dalí pursued his obsession with Millet's apparently idyllic painting *The Angelus,* described in the caption on page 28. In a 1938 essay, 'The Tragic Myth of Millet's Angelus', Dalí described how the female figure in the picture became identified in his mind with sexual aggression, her attitude suggesting that of the praying mantis, which devours the male after copulating with him. The fantastic rock shapes on the coast at Cape Creus, close to Dalí's home, suggested a transformation of Millet's couple into enormous menhirs, or statues. Though the male (on the left) is larger, he is already under assault from the long 'needle' approaching his neck, perhaps a metamorphosed version of the pitchfork in Millet's original.

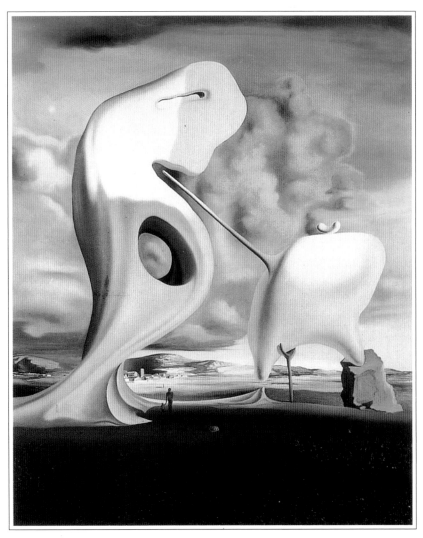

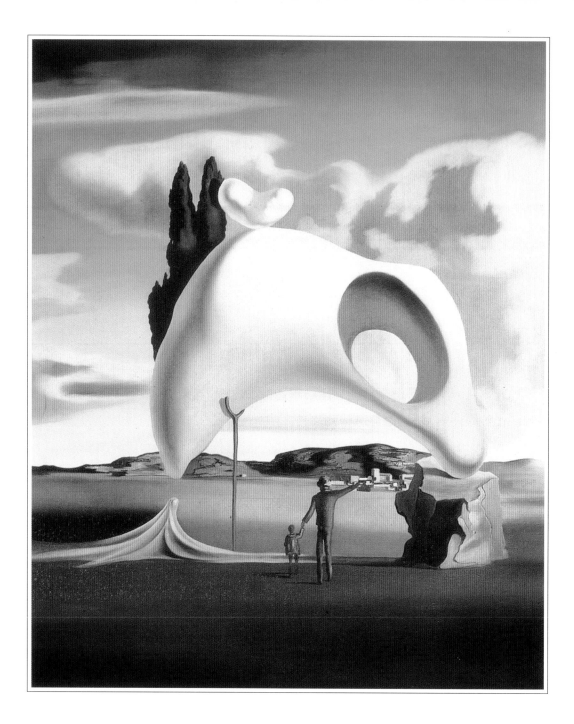

◁ **Atavistic Ruins after the Rain** 1934

Oil on canvas

THIS EVIDENTLY REPRESENTS a development of the scene in *The Architectonic Angelus of Millet* (page 29), in which the human figures have been metamorphosed into menhirs or sculptures. Actually they most closely resemble the sculptures of Dalí's contemporaries, Hans Arp and Henry Moore, but Dalí's treatment of them suggests that they are age-old rock formations. Dalí's own writings indicate that the 'remains' in this canvas are the result of erosion, but also of sexual conflict. The 'female' stone, which now dominates the picture, has devoured the male, in the process acquiring his characteristic void; all that remains of him is part of the display-like base of the object shown on page 29. The figures viewing the 'remains' represent the infant Dalí and his father, allied against the female sexuality of which Dalí had such a horror.

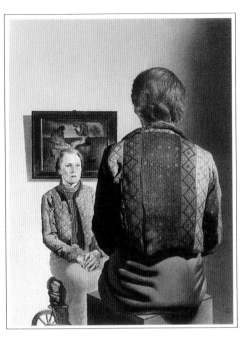

△ **Portrait of Gala** 1935

Panel

ALSO KNOWN, for obvious reasons, as *The Angelus of Gala:* behind her hangs a version of *The Angelus,* the painting by Millet that so obsessed Dalí (see pages 29 and 30); and the two people in the room – apparently front-Gala and back-Gala – are juxtaposed in roughly the same fashion as the peasants in the picture. But on this occasion Dalí has outrageously distorted Millet's composition, putting the peasants into a wheelbarrow (presumably as a form of erotic union) and altering the woman's attitude to increase the resemblance to a praying mantis that Dalí claimed to find in the original; presumably she is about to copulate with the man and then to devour him. By contrast, both Galas appear calm and untroubled, perhaps reflecting Dalí's conviction that she had been his saviour from sexual confusion and madness.

▷ **Mediumistic-Paranoiac Image** 1935

Oil on panel

BY THE TIME THIS WAS PAINTED, Dalí and Gala had formed a close relationship with the English collector Edward James, who contracted to buy the artist's entire output; the arrangement gave Dalí an assured income during the years when the Spanish Civil War (1936-9) had unsettled his life and he lived mainly in France. At one time James owned 40 important works by Dalí, including this one and a number of others illustrated in this book, for example *The Phantom Cart* (pages 26-27) and *Paranoiac-Critical Solitude* (pages 34-35). These were quite small (*Mediumistic-Paranoiac Image* is only 19 x 23 cm/7^1/$_2$ x 9 in), but Dalí also painted larger canvases, such as *Impressions of Africa* (pages 56-57), for James. Despite its title, *Mediumistic-Paranoiac Image* is almost Victorian in its realistic and innocently peaceful picture of the seaside, very much at odds with Dalí's normally subversive imagery.

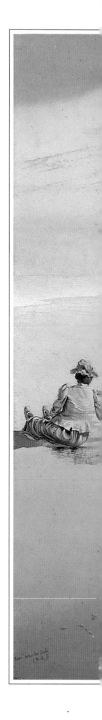

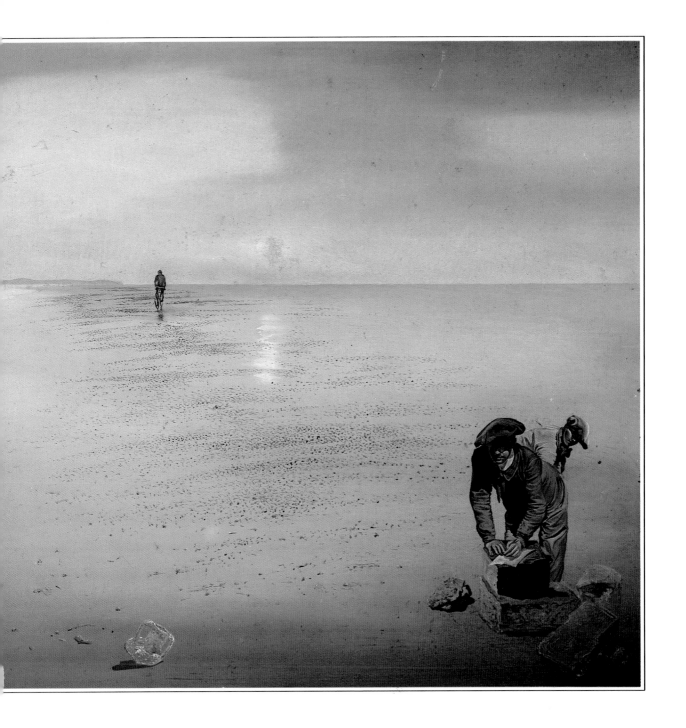

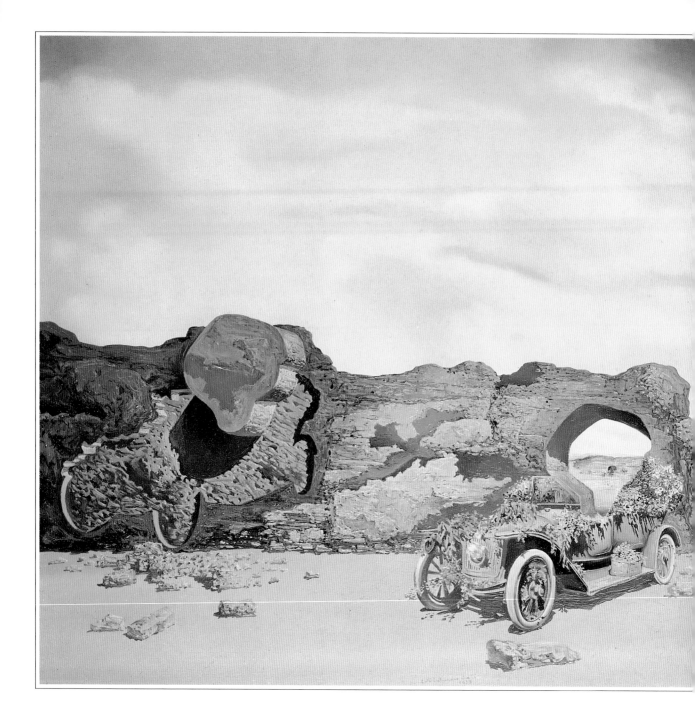

◁ **Paranoiac-Critical Solitude** 1935

Oil on panel

HERE DALI TRANSPOSES real objects to conjure up impossible relationships as part of his self-proclaimed crusade 'to discredit reality'. Mysteriously abandoned, a car has become overgrown with flowers and plants. It appears to be integrated into the rock behind it, and the missing parts of the windscreen and body correspond with the large hole above it; yet the car is solid and separate enough to cast a shadow on the ground. To the left, the shape of the car is impressed into the rock face, and above it a plug of rock projects which corresponds to the hole on the right. It is as if a single rock has split and opened up, revealing a 'fossil' automobile which has been imprisoned in it for ages of geological time, an attractive explanation that does not, however, account for all the visual contradictions that Dalí has incorporated into the scene.

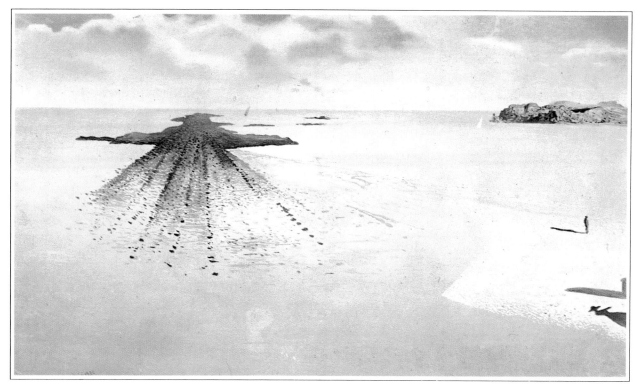

△ **Geological Justice** 1936

Oil on panel

LIKE *Mediumistic-Paranoiac Image* (pages 32-33), this is one of several small, cool paintings of empty beachscapes which Dalí painted for Edward James, who was supposed to be the artist's sole patron during this period. (In reality, Dalí's wife Gala sometimes cheated James by covertly selling paintings to other buyers.) The setting for these works was not Dalí's beloved Port Lligat, where he and Gala lived, but the nearby bay at Rosas, which had a very wide, flat beach. Although the scene looks perfectly natural and tranquil, the dark mud and stones form a figure resembling a steamrollered human figure, hence the original title, *Anthropomorphism Extra-Flat*. There is also a curiously sinister shadow on the right-hand edge of the scene, implying the presence of some possibly menacing figure. Nevertheless it is the atmospheric beauty of the work that remains uppermost in the viewer's mind.

▷ **Sun Table** 1936

Oil on panel

Like *Paranoiac-Critical Solitude*
(pages 34-35), *Sun Table* shows
Dalí moving away from purely
erotic and autobiographical
obsessions while continuing to
set his surreal encounters
against a local background, the
empty Ampurdán plain and
the coast around Cadaqués.
The table is a humdrum object
from a local café, supporting
three coffee-glasses and a
single coin. The tiles are a copy
of those that were being
installed in Dalí's Port Lligat
house. These are mysteriously
placed in a landscape with
beached boats and a stretch of
coastal sand that can evidently
be reinterpreted as desert. Or
at least that is what the
presence of the camel suggests.
Its egg-headed rider is faceless,
unlike the bust which, though
actually supported by a
column, seems to rest on the
camel's head. As on page 32, a
piece of ancient pottery lies in
the sand. Close to it, small but
unmistakable, is another
camel: on a pack of American
cigarettes of a particularly well-
known brand. The boy, seen in
silhouette, may represent Dalí.

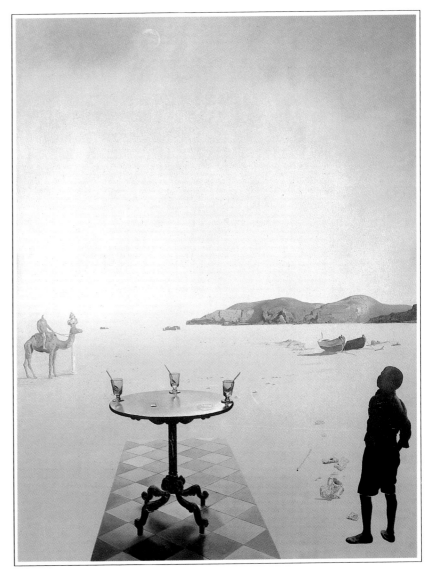

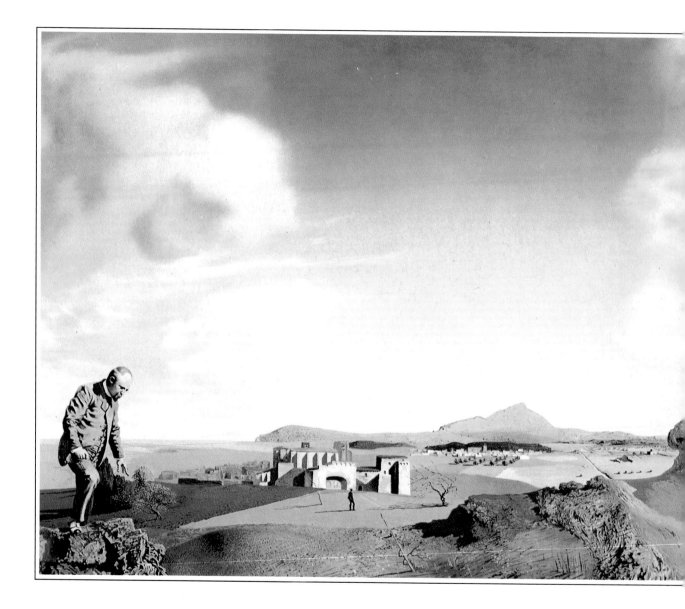

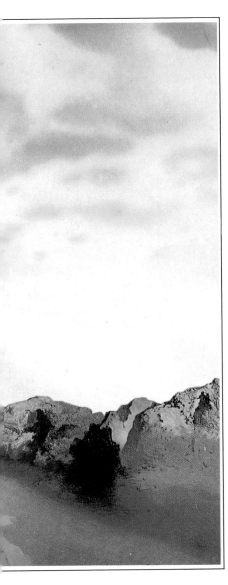

◁ The Chemist of Ampurdán Looking for Absolutely Nothing 1936

Oil on panel

THOUGH DALI'S IMAGE of him is spectre-like, the busy-about-nothing chemist was a real person, accurately depicted. Here he could well be a statue, like one of the mysterious monuments in the paintings of Paul Delvaux and Georges de Chirico, contemporaries who certainly influenced Dalí. The chemist makes another appearance in *Premonitions of Civil War* (page 42). The landscape is the Ampurdán plain as it appears in so many of Dalí's paintings, with its long perspectives and surrounding hills. As so often in his work, the title serves to undermine the content of the picture itself, making it irrational. Dalí pursued a similar strategy with regard to framing, insisting on putting pictures that were often quite small into ornate, heavy, old-fashioned frames which might initially deceive the spectator into believing that the subject would be treated in an equally traditional style.

Suburbs of a Paranoiac-Critical Town: Afternoon on the Outskirts of European History 1936

Oil on panel

▷ *Overleaf pages 40-41*

THIS IS A PAINTING of ingenious repeated images and neat dovetailing. In the foreground stands a cheerful Gala, holding up a bunch of grapes and welcoming the spectator into a scene that resembles three interlocked stage sets: all three were real places (the right-hand 'set' is the main street of Cadaqués). The grapes, the horse's skull and the statue's equine hindquarters are related shapes; but there are many more correspondences in the painting. The outline of the gateway behind Gala is a simplified version of the church tower that can be seen through it. The silhouette of the bell in the tower corresponds to that of the girl skipping in front of it. On the left-hand side of the panel, the low-domed structure, its high arcaded base and the two figures are reflected in the dressing-table, mirror and arch. Close by a miniature version sits on a soft open drawer.

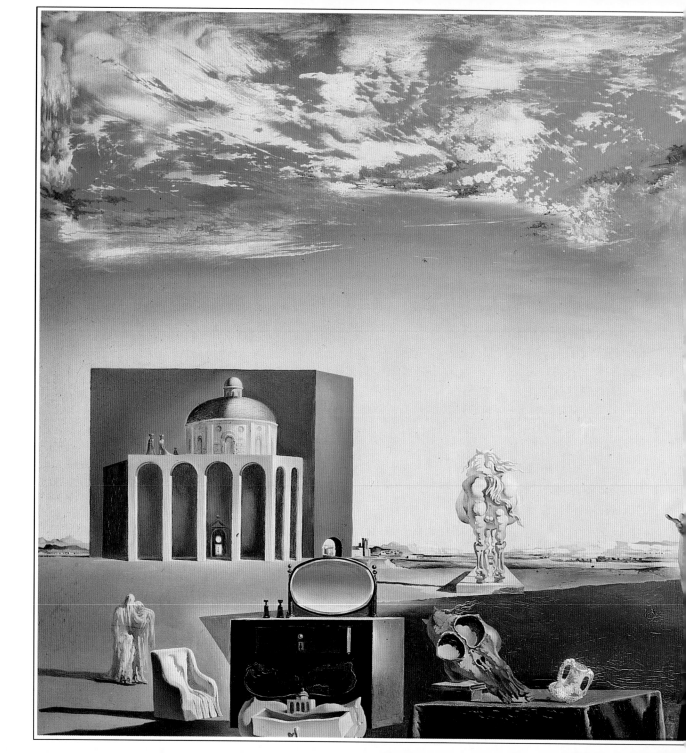

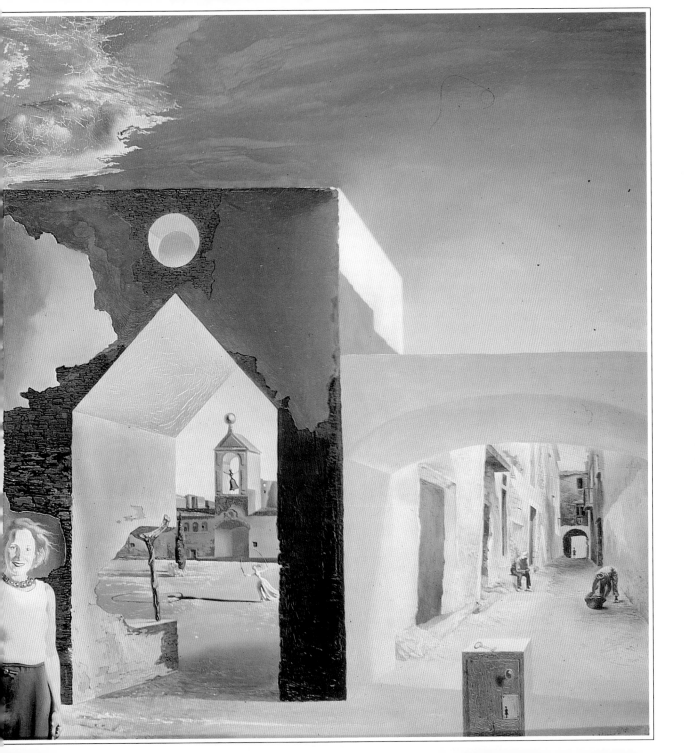

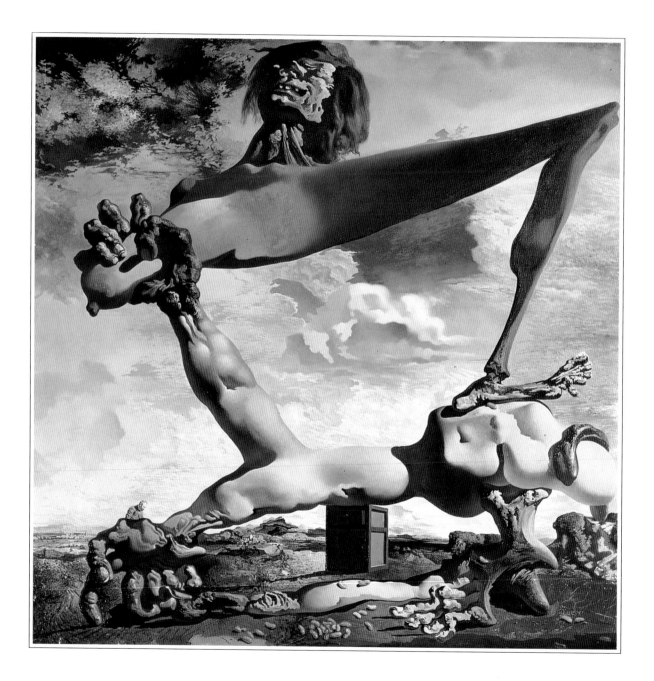

◁ **Soft Construction with Boiled Beans: Premonition of Civil War** 1936

Oil on canvas

DALI LIKED TO CLAIM that this celebrated picture proved his intuitive genius, since it was finished six months before the outbreak of the Spanish Civil War in July 1936. However, Spain had been in turmoil for some years, and the origins of *Premonition of Civil War* can be traced to Dalí's experiences during the 1934 separatist rising in Catalonia. Though Dalí's work owes something to his great Spanish predecessor, Goya, he nevertheless succeeded here in creating a potent image of national agony: a towering, monstrous figure, its limbs jumbled and distorted, tearing itself apart. Dalíesque logic equated self-devouring with dining conventions, and so the ruptured flesh must be served up with vegetables, hence the scattering of boiled beans. Above one of the monster's hands we glimpse the Ampurdán chemist (page 39) still seeking absolutely nothing.

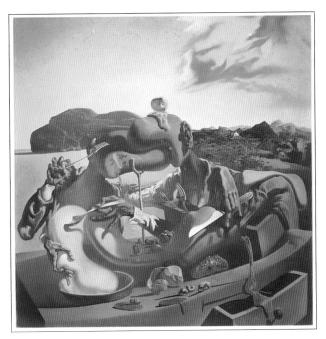

△ **Autumn Cannibalism** 1936

Oil on canvas

Autumn Cannibalism constitutes Dalí's response to the outbreak of the Spanish Civil War: a picture in which male and female carve up each other's flesh. However, the event is linked with the erotic obsessions so prominent in Dalí's earlier work, which reappear here in force. The cannibals are not fighting but kissing and embracing; the ants (a Dalí symbol of decay) are back; and the open drawer (another common Dalí image) implies the presence of the unconscious mind, a Pandora's box of unacceptable drives and impulses. Ironically, while Spain was being torn apart, Dalí was having a great success in the United States, dominating the Surrealist exhibition at New York's Museum of Modern Art and entering one version of the US Hall of Fame by appearing in December 1936 on the cover of Time magazine.

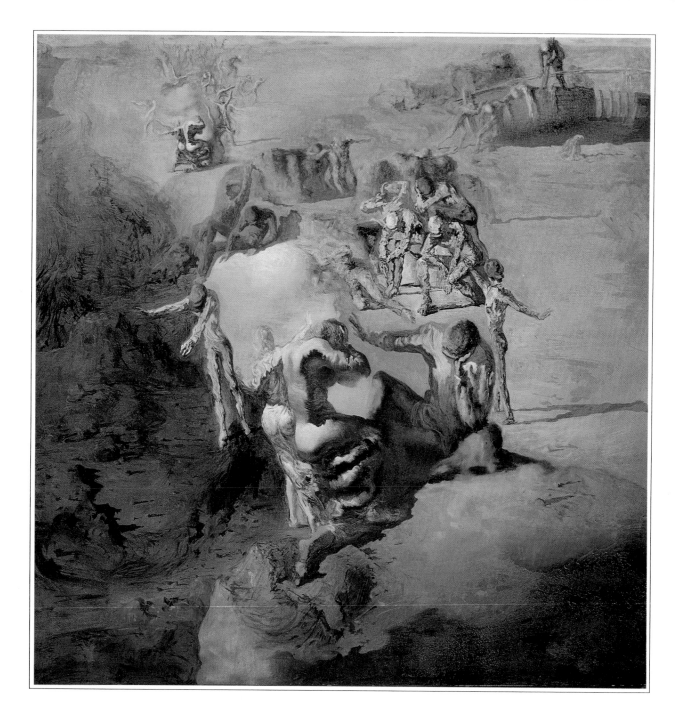

◁ **The Great Paranoiac** 1936

Oil on canvas

ONE OF DALI'S most stunning
double images, *The Great
Paranoiac* was painted after a
discussion between Dalí and a
fellow-artist, José Maria Sert,
on the work of Giuseppe
Arcimboldi, a 16th-century
Milanese painter celebrated
for portraits whose subjects
were composed entirely of
related objects (fruits, for
example, or weapons). In
similar fashion, but with more
dynamic results, Dalí's smiling
paranoiac dissolves into a
turbulent scene in which men
and women strike attitudes of
grief or dismay. The double
image is repeated, with
variations, in the background
to the left. To the right, by
contrast, a group of exhausted
figures seem to be trying to
haul a boat across the sand,
perhaps acting out one of the
delusions that seethe within
the brain of the Great
Paranoiac.

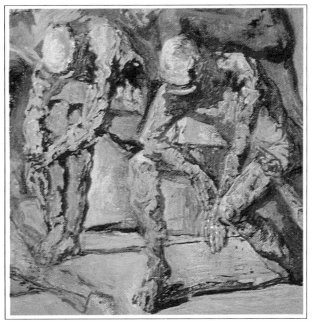

Detail

▷ **Swans Reflecting Elephants** 1937

Oil on canvas

THE HALLUCINATORY IMAGES created by Dalí's 'paranoiac-critical method' are of two main kinds: single images that change according to mysterious laws of perception, like *The Great Paranoiac* (page 44); and groups of two or more images that are unlike as subjects but are revealed as having disturbing visual affinities, for example the bell and the skipping girl in *Suburbs of a Paranoiac-Critical Town* (pages 40-41). But in this canvas Dalí has combined the two in a virtuoso display of illusionism. The swans and tree stumps, reflected in the water, somehow take on the appearance of elephants; yet when the picture is turned upside-down the swans are transformed into elephants and vice versa! The soft, slippery surfaces and writhing forms (even the clouds seem organic) create a distinctly uncomfortable atmosphere, apparently at odds with the presence of the prosaic, palely loitering man.

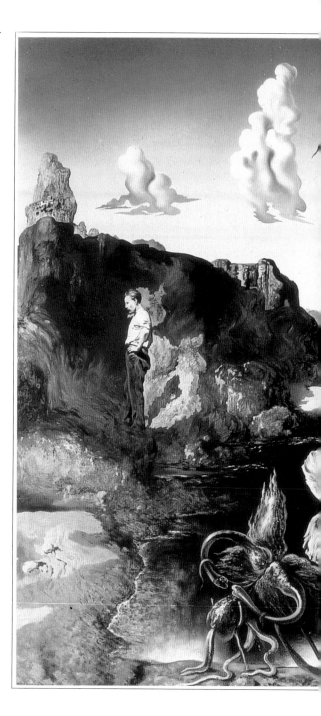

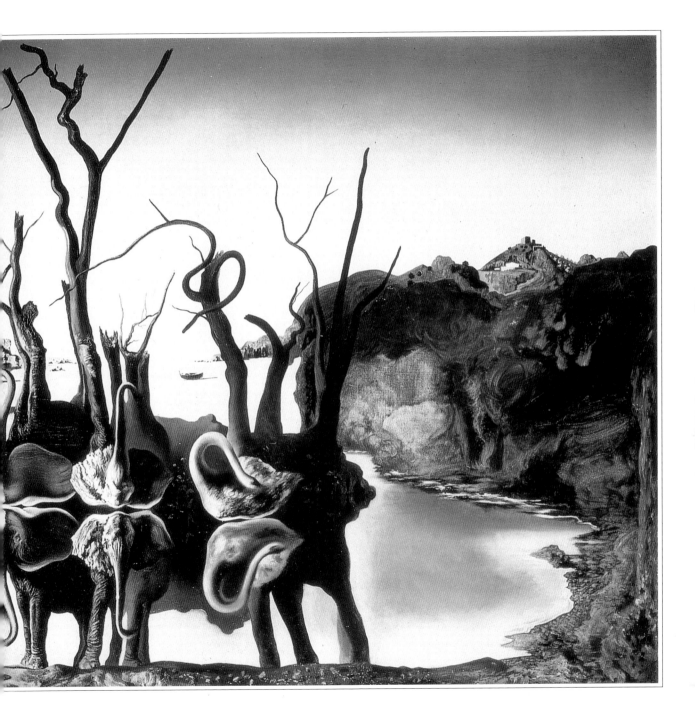

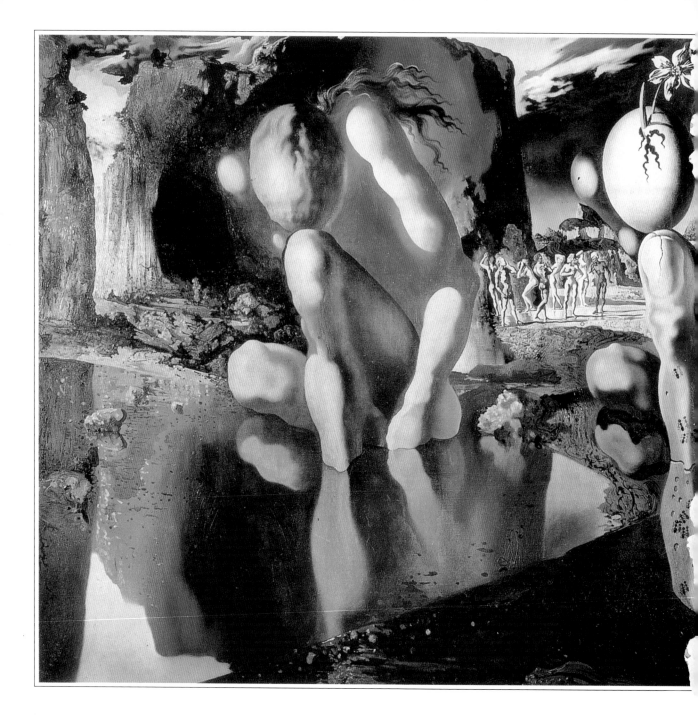

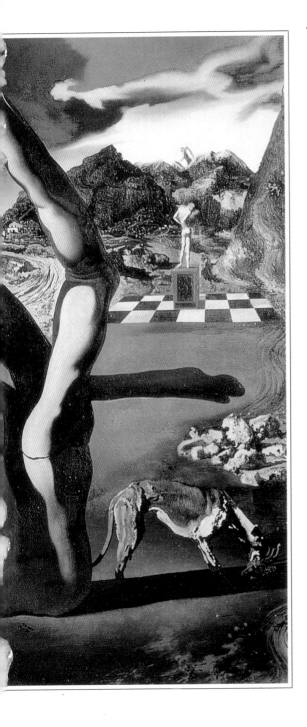

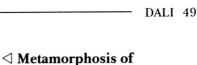

◁ **Metamorphosis of Narcissus** 1937

Oil on canvas

BACK IN PARIS after his great success in America, Dalí painted this picture and wrote a substantial poem to accompany it. In Greek myth, Narcissus was a surpassingly beautiful young man who saw his reflection in a fountain and fell in love with it. According to one version, unable to fulfil his desires, he pined away; but in a more dramatic alternative he leaned forward to embrace the image, toppled into the water and drowned. Afterwards the gods transformed him into the narcissus flower. Dalí shows Narcissus sitting in a pool, gazing down, while not far away there is a decaying stone figure which corresponds closely to him but is perceived quite differently – as a hand holding up a bulb or egg from which a narcissus is growing. In the background, a group of naked figures stand about attitudinizing, while a third narcissus-like figure appears on the horizon.

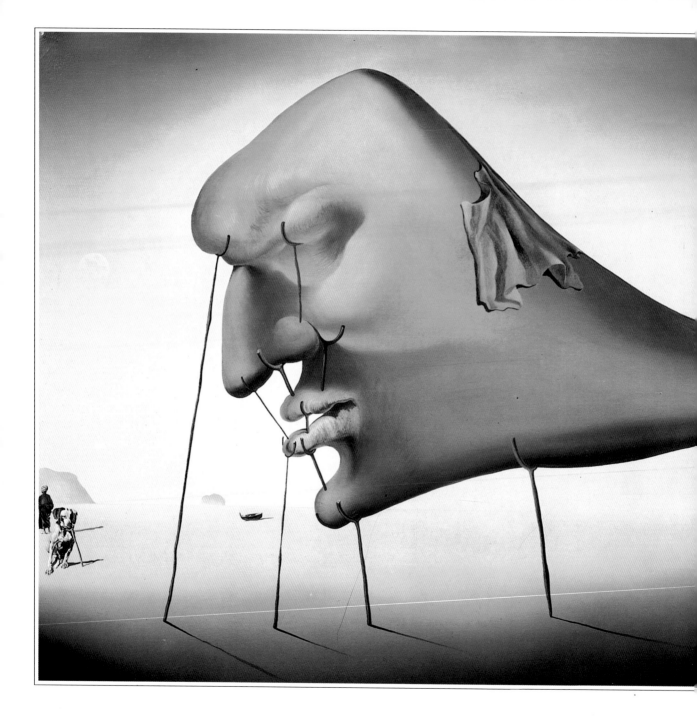

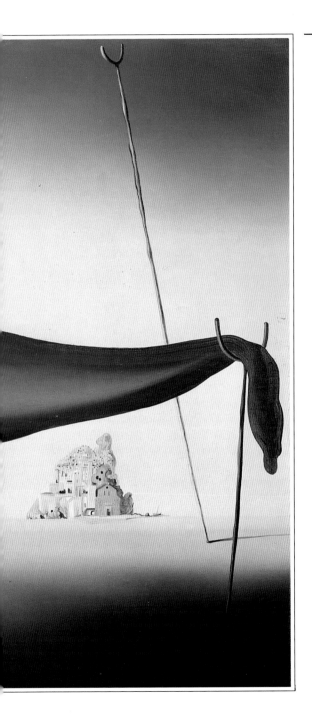

⊲ **Sleep** 1937

Oil on canvas

IN *Sleep,* Dalí recreated the kind of large, soft head and virtually non-existent body that had featured so often in his paintings around 1929. In this case, however, the face is certainly not a self-portrait. Sleep and dreams are *par excellence* the realm of the unconscious, and consequently of special interest to psychoanalyists and Surrealists. Dalí's sleeper – or personification of sleep – is appropriately troubled, and an extraordinary number of crutches are needed to support the head and precisely position each feature. Crutches had always been a Dalí trademark, hinting at the fragility of the supports which maintain 'reality', but here nothing seems inherently stable, and even the dog needs to be propped up! Everything in the picture except the head is bathed in a pale bluish light, completing the sense of alienation from the world of daylight and rationality.

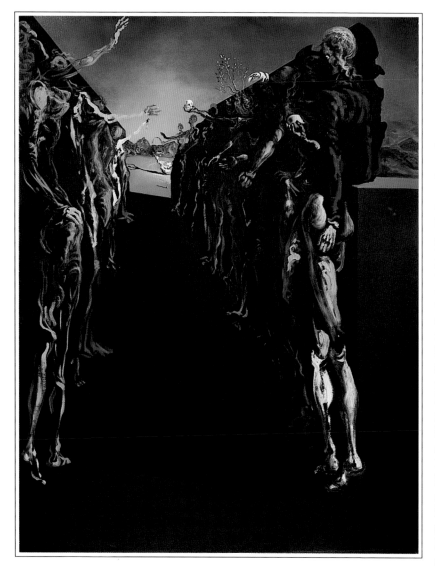

◁ **Palladio's Corridor of Thalia** 1937

Oil on canvas

DURING THE LATE 1930s Dalí spent long periods in Italy, where he made a careful study of Renaissance art. Among the masterpieces of the 16th-century architect Andrea Palladio was the Teatro Olimpico in Vicenza, in which both the theatre and the stage sets were modelled on ancient Roman examples. Here Dalí has devised an equivalent to Palladio's elaborate perspective effects by creating a receding corridor of human (if spectral) figures. The scene is divided into starkly contrasted dark and light areas, so that the corridor leads to the strongly lit figure of a girl playing with a skipping rope or hoop. This image had already appeared in *Suburb of a Paranoiac-Critical Town* (pages 40-41), and was based on a childhood memory of Dalí's cousin. Despite the innocent nature of her play, he somehow manages to make both the girl and her shadow as sinister as everything else in this curiously disturbing picture. Thalia was one of the nine Muses.

▷ **Spain** 1938

Oil on canvas

UNUSUALLY FOR DALI, the main image in this picture has a symbolic function which the artist himself draws attention to by painting in the title, *España* (Spain), at the bottom. Dalí's war-torn native land is represented by a woman whose head and upper torso can also be perceived as groups of fighting men; her lips correspond to the red cloak of one of the combatants, her nipples to the heads of two jousting horsemen. Both the woman's face and the fighters are painted in a style reminiscent of Leonardo da Vinci – appropriately enough, since Leonardo anticipated Dalí (and psychoanalysis) in recommending the study of moss, stains and cloud formations as stimuli from which the imagination could draw inspiration for new subjects. In his work, Dalí remained apolitical, dwelling on the self-devouring nature of the Spanish Civil War; in his life he was more opportunistic, becoming increasingly enthusiastic about General Franco as the Fascist forces advanced.

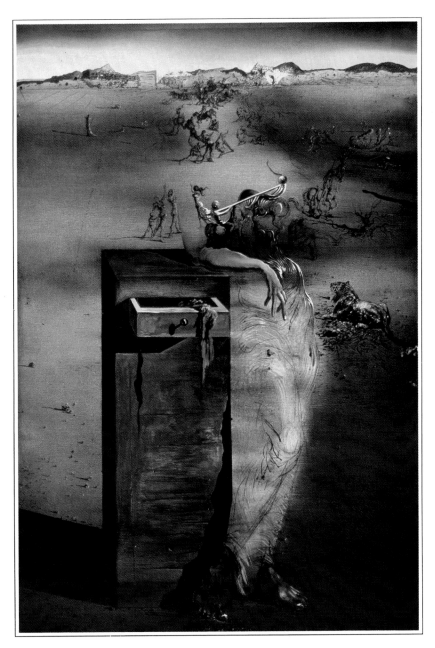

▷ **Mountain Lake** 1938

Oil on canvas

LIKE MANY OF HIS contemporaries, Dalí responded with alarm to the wars and threats of wars that plagued civilization in the late 1930s. According to Dalí himself, in *Mountain Lake* the telephone represents the apparatus used by Britain's prime minister, Neville Chamberlain, to negotiate with Hitler; at that date it was still a novel instrument of diplomacy. The fragility of the process is indicated by the presence of a crutch, and by the fact that the line has been cut. However, Dalí's political interpretation of the canvas smacks of hindsight, since in 1938 Chamberlain appeared to have achieved 'peace in our time' through the Munich agreement. The purely personal element in the painting remains strong, expressed through the striking double image of the lake, which can equally well be viewed as a fish on a slab or a male sexual organ!

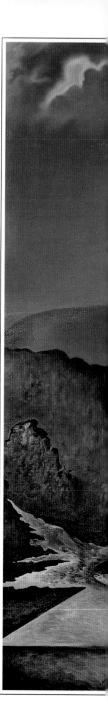

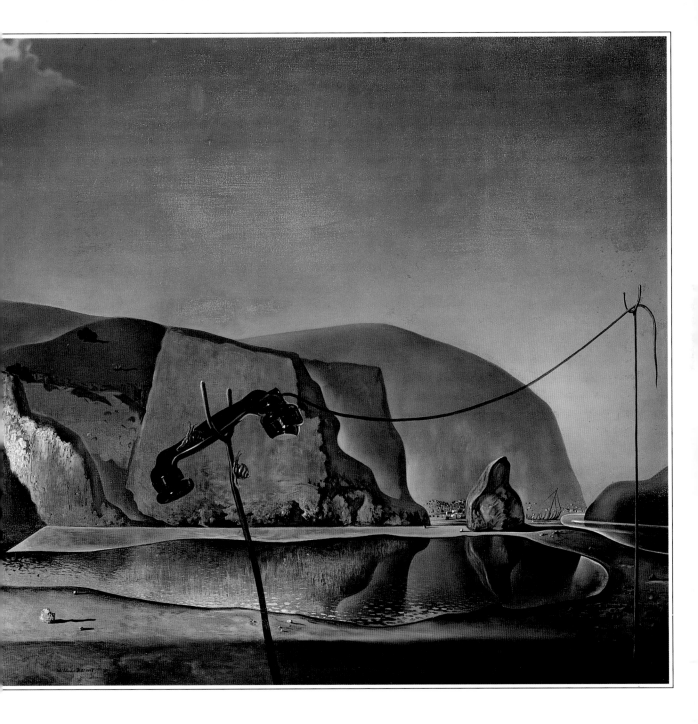

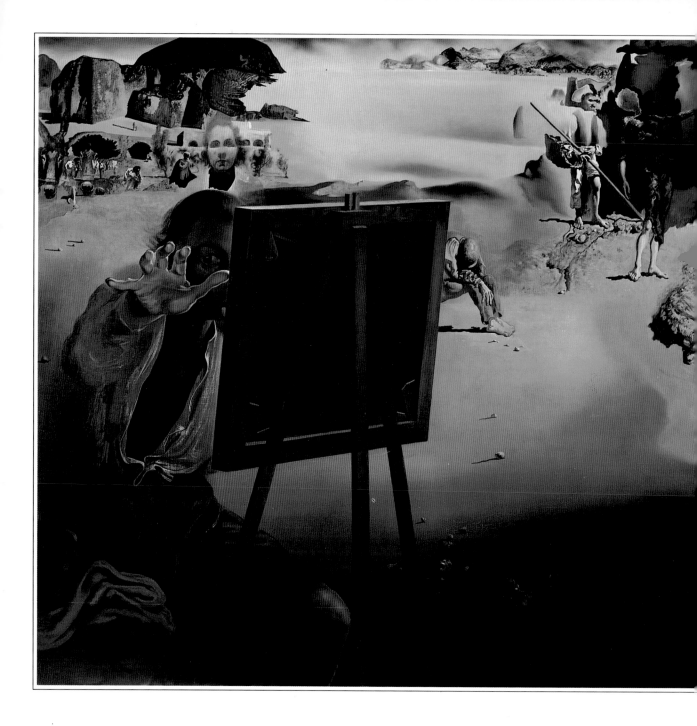

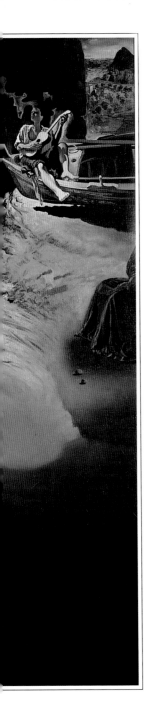

◁ **Impressions of Africa** 1938

Oil on canvas

THIS IS NOTABLE FOR the self-portrait of Dalí in front of his easel, staring fixedly in an effort to summon up images from his unconscious to transfer straight on to the canvas. His foreshortened hand, flung out at the spectator, is reminiscent of the 17th-century master Caravaggio, one of the Italian masters whom Dalí was diligently studying in the late 1930s. Typically Dalíesque double images are crowded into the back of the picture, including his wife Gala with eyes in shadow that can be interpreted as part of an arcade, and an image of a priest which also resembles a donkey's head. The African aspect of the work can be evaluated on the basis of Dalí's statement that 'Africa counts for something in my work, since without having been there I remember it so well!'

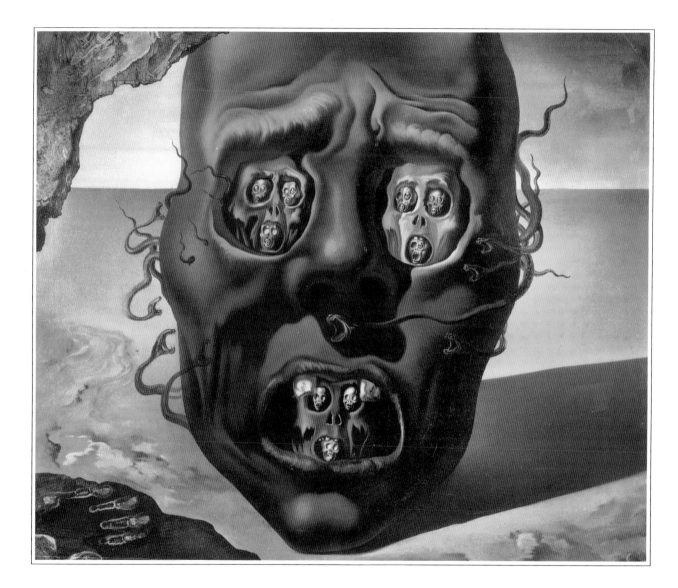

◁ **The Face of War** 1940

Oil on canvas

The Face of War was painted in the United States, where Dalí was to live for eight years and reach the pinnacle of his worldly fame and success. In the summer of 1940 he and his wife fled from France, whose armies were collapsing in the face of the German invasion, and, like so many refugees, sailed via Lisbon to the New World. The meaning of the painting is, for Dalí, unusually straightforward, employing symbolism rather than the irrational associations of the 'paranoiac-critical method'. A skull-like head surrounded by long, hissing snakes has every orifice filled with skeletons; each skeleton contains skeletons and skeletons-within-skeletons, so that the head is 'stuffed with infinite death', a potent symbol of the age of concentration camps and mass murders.

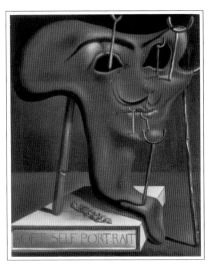

△ **Soft Self-Portrait with Grilled Bacon 1941**

Oil on canvas

USUALLY MOST IN EARNEST when dwelling on the subject of his own genius, Dalí has here caricatured his public image in a spirit of gentle self-mockery. His identity is mainly conveyed by the upturned, antenna-like moustaches which made his appearance instantly memorable. Crutches are an even more familiar presence in his work, and Dalí himself noted that the public, instead of growing tired of them, seemed to become more and more enthusiastic as he multiplied their numbers; so he has drawn the appropriate conclusion, using crutches large, medium and small to prop up his helplessly soft self-image on all sides. The ants round eye and mouth also signify decay or weakness. The grilled bacon lies in front of the self-portrait, which is made of a material which might well be excrement.

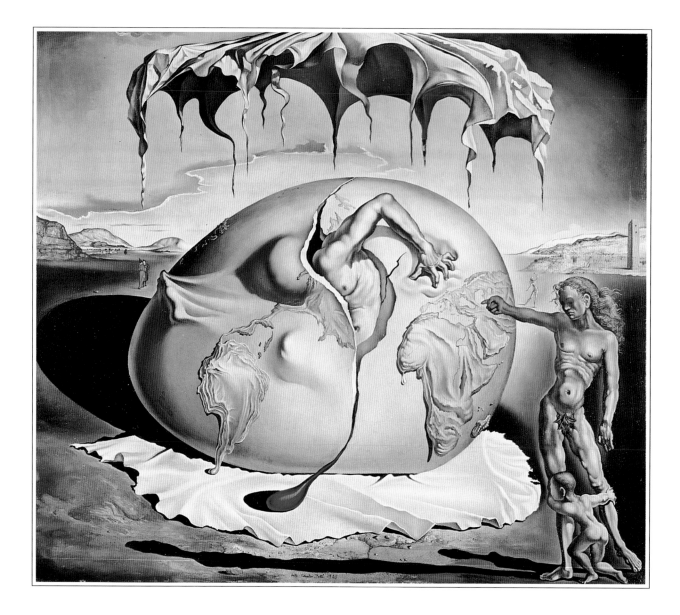

▷ **Geopoliticus Child Watching the Birth of the New Man** 1943

Oil on canvas

THE TITLE OF THIS PAINTING sounds like a parody of all the optimistic predictions made during World War II of the 'new world' that would emerge after the defeat of fascism. Geopolitics was a study, fashionable in the 1930s, which focused on the geographical factors influencing the destinies of states, and especially their location on the great continental land masses. The presence of a child watching the 'birth' of a grown man serves to undermine the concept and strengthen the viewer's scepticism, which Dalí shared. Like a chicken, the New Man is breaking out of the globe, which has a soft skin rather than a shell. Even the continents are soft and apparently on the point of oozing away; mysteriously, West Africa has shed a teardrop. The spiky canopy and the pointing woman, at once muscular and emaciated, help to give the picture its rather forbidding atmosphere.

Sentimental Colloquy 1944

Oil on canvas

▷ *Overleaf pages 62-63*

ON OCCASION, Dalí liked to claim that painting was the least significant aspect of his genius. It was certainly true that he assumed a great variety of roles, especially after his successes in the United States gave him abundant opportunities. He was, among other things, an inventor, a fashion and jewellery designer, a writer, a movie-set designer (Alfred Hitchcock's *Spellbound*), as well as a self-publicist, an early exponent of performance art and eventually the 'star' of many TV commercials. In 1944 Dalí wrote his only novel, *Hidden Faces*, worked with Hitchcock, and designed the sets for *Sentimental Colloquy*, a ballet loosely based on one of Verlaine's poems. Staged in New York, *Sentimental Colloquy* was a Surrealist extravaganza featuring dancers with underarm hair hanging down to the floor, a large mechanical tortoise encrusted with coloured lights, and the manic cyclists commemorated in this painting of the event.

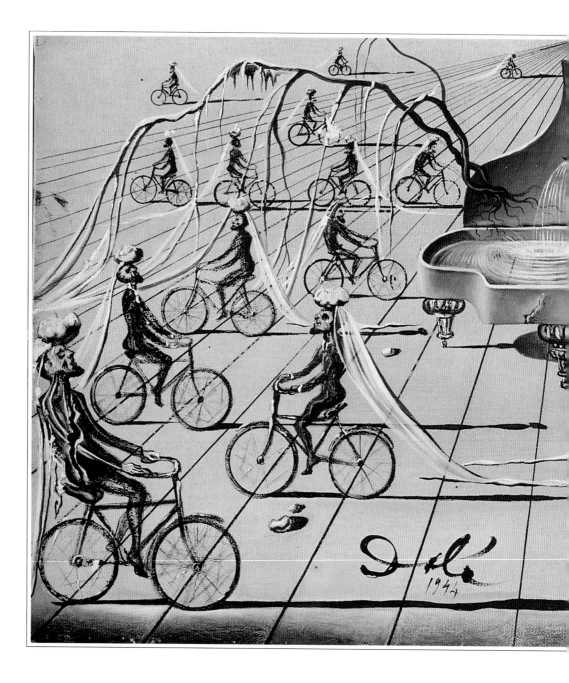

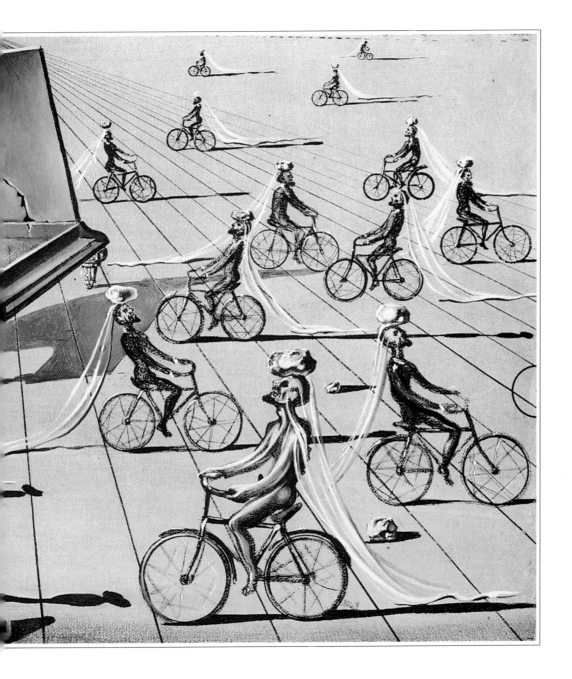

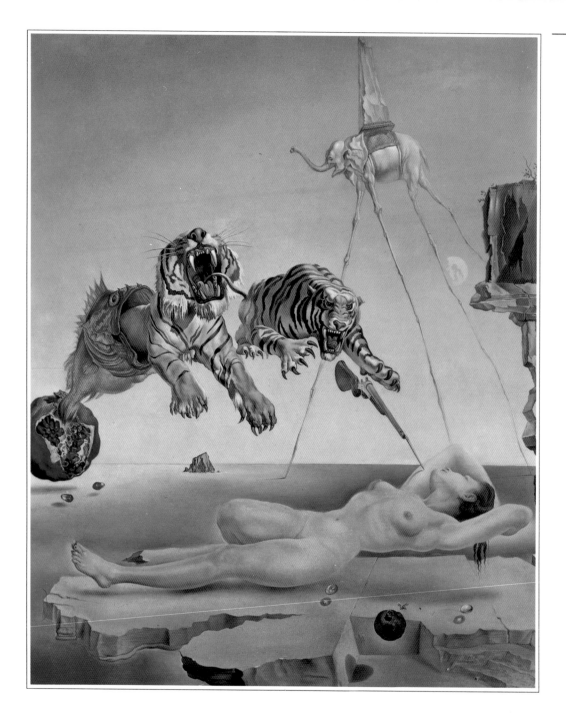

◁ Dream Caused by the Flight of a Bee around a Pomegranate One Second before Waking Up 1944

Oil on canvas

ONE SOURCE for this painting was a poster image of circus tigers, and Dalí has retained much of the bright immediacy associated with poster art. The bee and pomegranate referred to in the title are quite small objects, just below the outstretched body of the sleeping woman. She is obviously yet another portrait of Dalí's wife Gala, shown floating above (rather than resting on) a stone ledge, surrounded by the sea of the unconscious. The 'real' bee and pomegranate are dwarfed by the images they have brought into being: a huge pomegranate, the fish that has burst out of it, and the two tigers, depicted in all their snarling ferocity, which erupt from the fish's mouth. A more orthodox Freudian image, the rifle with fixed bayonet, and the fantastic elephant with stilt-legs, complete the one-second dream, which has apparently not had time to disturb the sleeper's tranquillity.

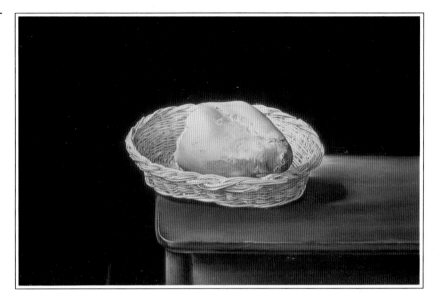

△ The Basket of Bread 1945

Oil on canvas

IN 1941 DALI announced that he intended 'to become classic', a development foreshadowed by his study of Italian Renaissance artists, and one which perhaps reflected a feeling that he had exhausted psychic autobiography. From this time he turned increasingly to the outside world as a source of inspiration, although he continued to interpret it in 'paranoiac-critical' fashion. Unlike most pioneers of modern art, Dalí had always produced highly finished works, and in the 1940s his style approximated still more closely to the 19th-century 'academic' ideal, widely regarded at that time as utterly outmoded. The pull of tradition, which became increasingly strong, can be seen in this superbly painted, apparently simple work, in which the bread and basket seem lit from within, floating in darkness. The subject had been tackled by Dalí 20 years earlier, attracting him partly because of its affinities with the work of admired Spanish masters such as Velázquez and Zurbarán. Here it also foreshadows Dalí's ventures into religious painting from the 1950s.

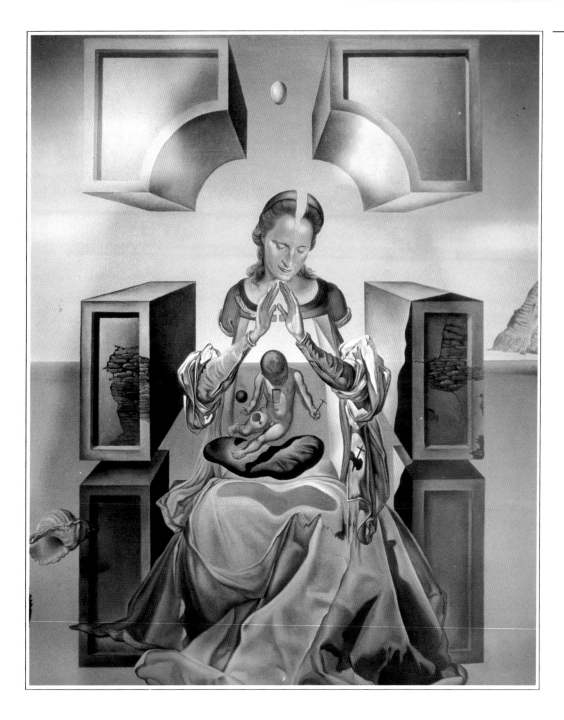

◁ **First Study for the Madonna of Port Lligat** 1949

Oil on canvas

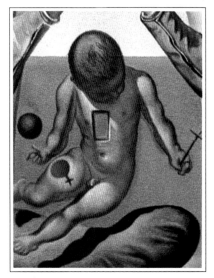

Detail

DALI FINALLY RETURNED to Spain in 1948, although by this time he was an international celebrity and would continue to spend a good deal of his time abroad. At Port Lligat he set to work on a Madonna, completed in 1950, which marks the beginning of his religious phase. The picture illustrated here is actually a highly finished preliminary study, but arguably its quiet emotion is more effective than the grandiosity of the final version. The Madonna was blessed by Pope Pius XII, to whom Dalí was presented in 1949. Dalí had already made a cult of his wife Gala as a semi-divine being, so there was an unseemly element in his portrayal of her as the Madonna, even leaving out of account her own marked taste for young men and large sums of money that were not always honestly come by. The influence of Renaissance art on Dalí's work was now at its height. The fragmentation of images in the picture reflects the 'nuclear mysticism' that is also apparent in *Exploding Raphaelesque Head* (page 68) and other works.

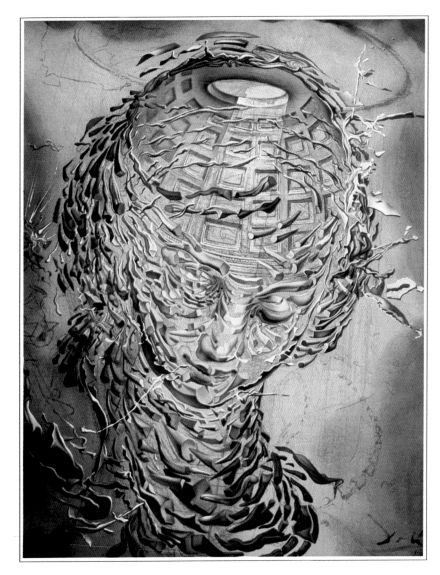

◁ **Exploding Raphaelesque Head** 1951

Oil on canvas

THE FRAGMENTED FORMS which appear in this painting and on page 66, originated in Dalí's study of nuclear physics. Deeply impressed by the discoveries which led to the development of the atomic bomb, he embraced 'nuclear painting' and 'nuclear mysticism'. Whatever their theoretical merits (or otherwise), these notions led to the creation of works of art in which Dalí's originality was very much to the fore. The head is like one of Raphael's Madonnas, classically pure and serene; at the same time it incorporates the interior of the dome of the Pantheon in Rome, with the light shining down through it. Both images are perfectly clear in spite of the explosion, which has blown the entire structure into small fragments shaped like rhinoceros horns, a new Dalí obsession most fully expressed on page 73. In the bottom left-hand corner, the fragments coalesce into a wheelbarrow, long an erotic symbol in Dalí's work.

▷ **Christ of St John of the Cross** 1951

Oil on canvas

A FAMOUS AND POPULAR painting, although there was a good deal of controversy when Glasgow Art Gallery decided to buy it in 1952. Its main source was a drawing made by the Spanish mystic St John of the Cross after a visionary experience. It showed the crucifixion, most unusually, from above, and according to Dalí this fused with his own 'cosmic dream' involving a sphere fitted into a triangle (Christ's head and the triangle formed by his arms and the line of the cross). The crucifixion takes place high over the rocky shores close to Dalí's home; but such an 'unhistorical' shift in time and place is common and acceptable in religious art, serving to emphasize the timeless, universal character of the New Testament narrative.

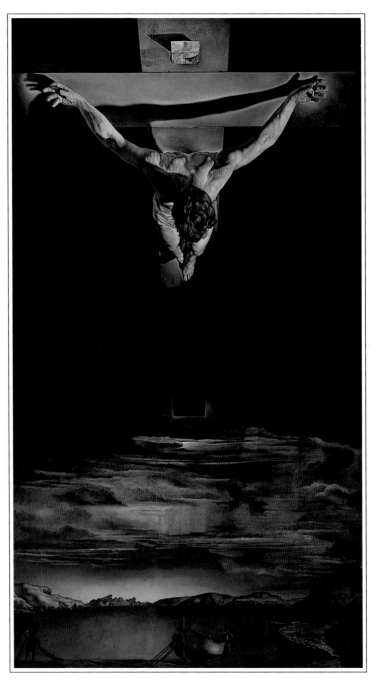

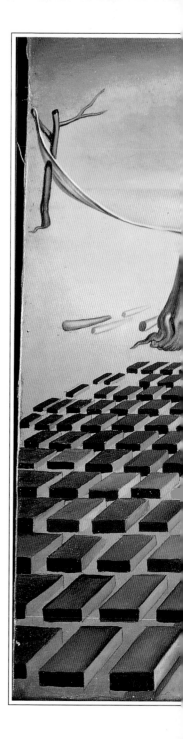

▷ **The Disintegration of the Persistence of Memory** 1952-4

Oil on canvas

DALI'S REWORKING of his famous *Persistence of Memory* (pages 20-21) is done in the spirit of the 'nuclear mysticism' displayed on pages 66 and 68. 'Persistence' and 'disintegration' might seem to be mutually exclusive, but not in the paranoiac-critical universe of Salvador Dalí. The soft watches are quietly falling apart, but much of the world about them seems to be fragmenting with production-line precision into geometric blocks; the straightened horns hint at the mathematical wonders of the rhinoceros (page 73). Most of the scene is under the water, which Dalí turns into a kind of skin, hanging from a branch; in other paintings it can be lifted like a sheet to reveal the sea-bed. Beneath the fish lies a transparent, near-extinct version of the self-portrait head that appears in so many works of the late 1920s and early 1930s.

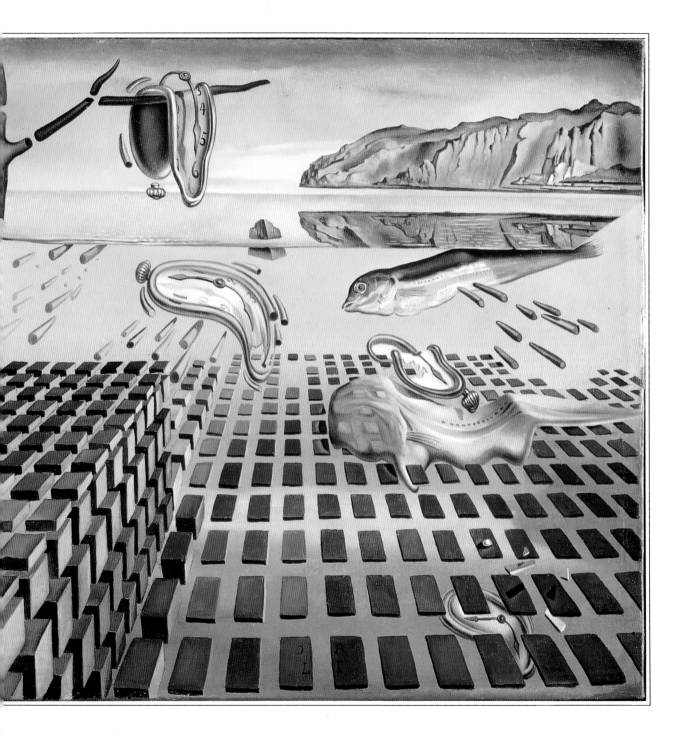

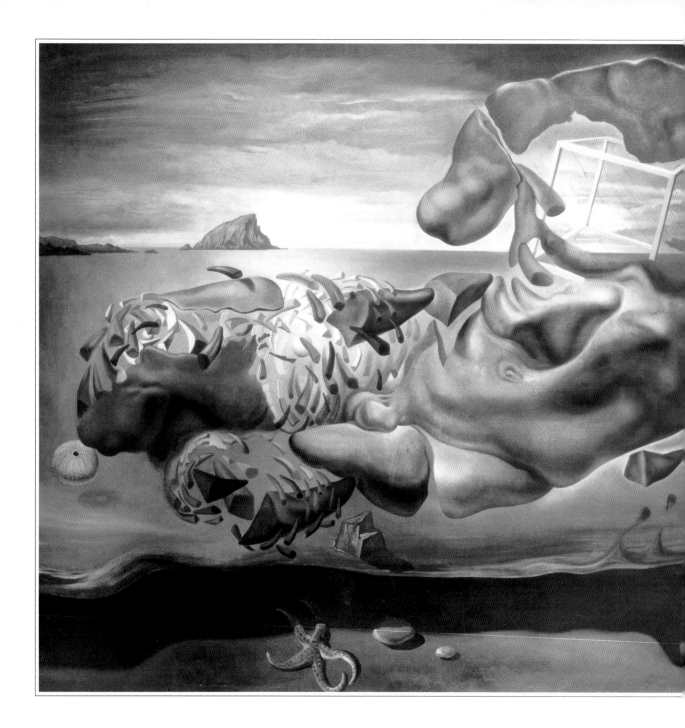

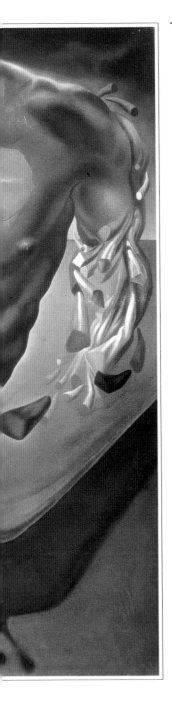

◁ **Rhinocerotic Figure of Phidias's Illisos** 1954

Oil on canvas

THIS COMES FROM what Dalí described as his 'almost divine and chaste rhinoceros-horn period', when he claimed that the curve of the beast's horn was the only perfect logarithmic spiral and consequently the ultimate in formal perfection. With characteristic Dalíesque logic – or critical paranoia – this insight came to him while he was copying a canvas that had obsessed him for decades: Vermeer's cool, lovely, light-filled portrait of a lacemaker.

In the mid-1950s Dalí even made a film called *The Prodigious Story of the Lacemaker and the Rhinoceros*, starring himself, a reproduction of the Vermeer, and a live, if carefully fenced-off, rhino. Here a torso from the Parthenon by the most famous of ancient Greek sculptors, Phidias, is fragmenting into a rhino head and horn-shapes which hang above a typical Dalí seascape, which is in turn suspended over the sea-bed.

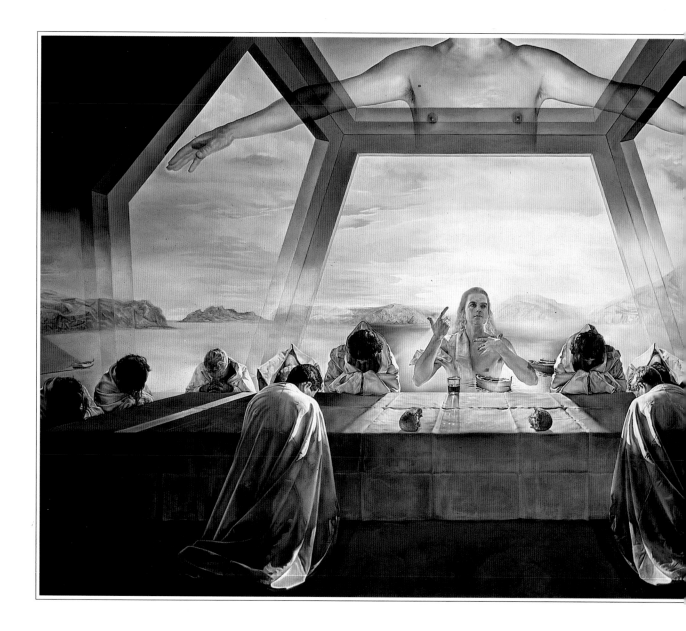

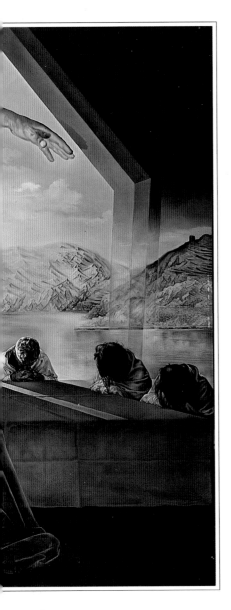

◁ **The Last Supper** 1955

Oil on canvas

LIKE OTHER RELIGIOUS paintings by Dalí, *The Last Supper* provokes widely divergent reactions: some critics have denounced it as slick and banal, while others believe that Dalí has succeeded in revitalizing the traditional imagery of devotion. The controversies were complicated by public awareness of Dalí as a personality, apparently more interested in intellectual and emotional games-playing than expressing genuine convictions. Jesus and his 12 disciples are assembled within a modernistic, glass-encased room. The disciples, their heads bowed, kneel round a large stone table, their solid forms contrasting with the transparency of Christ. Two pieces of bread and a half-full glass of wine represent the sacramental meal. Dalí constructed this picture according to mathematical principles derived from his study of the Renaissance, and Leonardo da Vinci (who painted the most famous of Last Suppers) is a particularly strong influence. With a rather Leonardo-like gesture, Jesus points towards heaven and the figure (perhaps the Holy Ghost) whose arms stretch out to embrace the company.

▷ **Tuna Fishing** 1966-7

Oil on canvas

A VERY LARGE CANVAS, crammed with violent action, *Tuna Fishing* has an epic character that is unusual in Dalí's work. Its extraordinary photographic quality is a tribute to his skill, and also to his modernity in using a projector to place directly on to the canvas the images he wished to copy. The images themselves range from Hellenistic sculpture to the cinema. The slaughter of the fish is shown as a bloodbath which might equally well be a gladiatorial scene. The straining muscles and violent postures of the men are like figures by Michelangelo, heroically intense and glorying in the kill; by contrast, the authentic fishermen in the background are (literally) less colourful, going about their business with professional detachment. Also in the background, but by no means inconspicuous, a naked woman attracts unaccountably little attention.

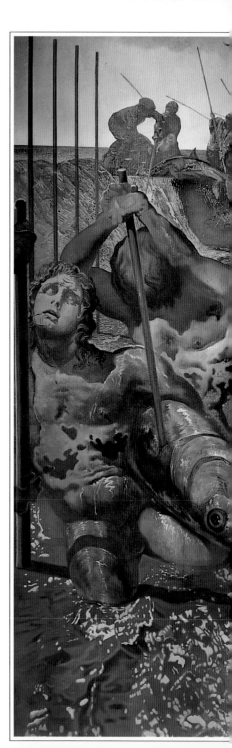

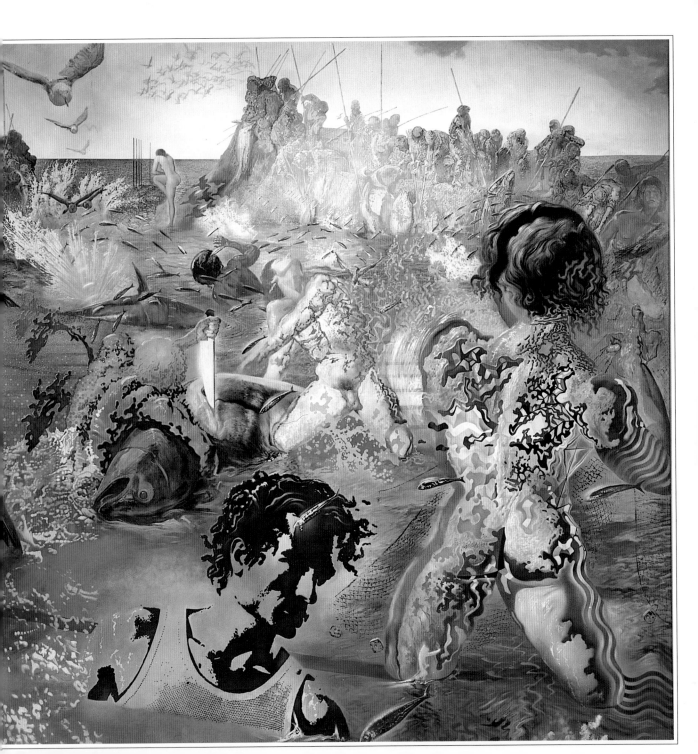

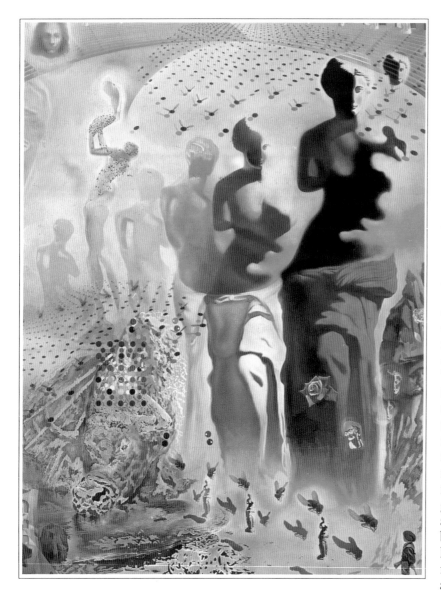

◁ **The Hallucinogenic Toreador** 1968-70

Oil on canvas

THE ARTIST HIMSELF called this huge canvas, suggested by a box of Venus pencils, 'All Dalí in one painting', for it comprises an anthology of Dalíesque images. At its top, a spiritualised head of Gala Dalí presides over the scene; in the bottom right-hand corner stands six-year-old Dalí, straight out of *The Spectre of Sex Appeal* (page 24). As well as many small images from earlier works, there is a Venus de Milo series in which the figure turns in the other direction and changes sex. The toreador himself is hard to make out at first, until we realize that the bare torso of the second Venus from the right can be interpreted as a face (her right breast as a nose, the shadow across her midriff as a mouth) and the green shadow on her drapery as a tie. To the left is the bullfighter's glittering 'suit of lights', which merges into rocks which can also be seen as the head of a dying bull. A metamorphical *tour de force!*

ACKNOWLEDGEMENTS

The Publisher would like to thank the following for their kind permission to reproduce the paintings in this book:

Bridgeman Art Library, London/Christie's, London 16-17, 32-33; /**Dali Museum, Beachwood, Ohio** 78; /**Davlyn Gallery, New York** 25; /**Ex-Edward James Foundation, Sussex** 26, 34-35, 36, 37, 38-39, 40-41, 44, 46-47, 48-49, 50-51, 52, 56-57; /**Index, Barcelona** 8-9; /**Index/Marquette University Fine Art Committee, Milwaukee** 66; /**Index/Museo Dali, Figueras** 65; /**Index/Private Collection** 15, 24, 59, 68, 70-71, 72-73; /**Juan Casanelles Collection** 13, **Luis Bunuel Collection** 10; /**Museo de Arte Contemporaneo, Madrid** 11; /**Museo Espanol de Arte Contemporaneo, Madrid** 12; /**Museum Boymans-van Beuningen, Rotterdam** 53, 58; /**Museum of Modern Art, New York** 20-21, 31, /**National Gallery of Art, Washington D.C.** 74-75; /**National Gallery of Canada , Ottawa** 28; /**Paul Ricard Foundation, Bandol, France** 76-77; /**Perls Gallery, New York** 30; /**Perslys Galleries, New York** 29; /**Philadelphia Museum of Art, Pennsylvania, USA** 42; /**Private Collection** 14, 9, 22, 62-63; /**Reynold Morse Collection** 60-61; /**Tate Gallery, London** 43, 54-55; /**Thyssen-Bornemisza Collection, Madrid** 64; /**Von der Heydt Musuem, Wuppertal** 23.